The Course Leader's Cookbook

The Course Leader's Cookbook

with Recipes for Successful Learning Experiences

Richard D. Colvin & Naomi C. Steinberg

Illustrated by Robert Stanley

San Diego • Toronto • Amsterdam • Sydney

Copyright © 1985, 1990

THE LEARNING EXPERIENCE

ISBN: 0-88390-303-2
Printed in the United States of America
All rights reserved

> The text of this publication, or any part thereof, may not
> be reproduced or transmitted in any form by any means,
> electronic or mechanical, including photocopying,
> recording, storage in an information retrieval system, or
> otherwise, without prior written permission.

Published by

8517 Production Avenue
San Diego, California 92121
(619) 578-5900, Fax (619) 578-2042

Foreword

When I first spoke with Dick Colvin about our special problem of having to rely on nonprofessional trainers to conduct Manufacturing Leadership Curriculum courses at more than 20 General Electric locations, little did I expect the result to be a "cookbook."

The term "cookbook" usually has a negative connotation in management development and training circles — we hear so often, "There is no 'cookbook' answer; no 'one right way' to do things" — which is perfectly true. But, as we point out in this book, there are certain practices that form the basis for effective results.

The metaphor of a cookbook is very appropriate. The experienced chef works from a library of basic recipes and what he or she does to enhance these recipes is what distinguishes a great chef from one who is mediocre. Our many years of creating learning experiences for supervisors, managers and trainers, have proved to us that there are underlying key practices which will ensure effective course leadership. And, if these are followed, a reasonably good class will result. However, just as with the experienced chef, the effective course leader adds to these key practices; experiments with different ingredients; modifies the amount and types of "seasonings"; makes effective use of all ingredients, particularly the knowledge and experience of the group.

The experienced course leader knows that he or she can't "teach" — *only help people learn.* Our dilemma was: what can we do to help people who are not trainers lead packaged courses in a way that helps the participants learn. For the most part, the course leaders are operating managers and technical or professional experts; the course leading is in addition to their regular duties. Most do not have the time to attend formal train-the-trainer sessions or do extensive research on how to conduct a class. We looked at the available literature and found that, for the most part, it was aimed at the professional or soon-to-be-professional trainer. There was really nothing in a how-to format to meet our need.

The Course Leader's Cookbook contains practical advice on how to create learning experiences. It does not dwell on theory, but provides solid, down-to-earth practices. It talks about what tools and techniques are available to the course leader and how to use them effectively. It provides concrete examples — the "recipes" — for various types of classroom activities ranging from lecture to small-group activities and individual learning situations. It encourages course leaders to use these as the foundation of their repertoire and to build on them, to experiment and to try new combinations. It also provides solid information on how to effectively use questions — the most important tool of all for creating successful learning experiences.

All in all, I'm convinced that *The Course Leader's Cookbook* is the only one of its kind: an easy-to-use, generic reference for nonprofessional course leaders.

                      Naomi C. Steinberg
                      Technical Education Operation
                      General Electric Company
                      Bridgeport, CT

Table of Contents

WORDS OF ENCOURAGEMENT ix

METHODS 1
   Lecture 2
   Discussion 4
      Information-Gathering 4
      Experience-Sharing 5
      Case Study 5
      Setting the Climate 6
   Experiential 8
      Role-Play 9
      Games 10
      Simulations 10
      Creating "A-Ha's" 11
      Laboratories 12
      Interactive Personal Computer 13
      Interactive Video 13

INGREDIENTS 15
   Lesson Plan 15
   Course Leader's Knowledge 16
   Participants' Knowledge and Experience 17

Table of Contents

Questioning 17
   To Introduce Topics 19
   To Get Examples/Experiences 20
   To Get More Information 20
   To Get Clarification 21
   To Follow Up 21
   To Test Understanding 21
   To Test for Application 22

Examples 22

Demonstration 23

Small-Group Activities 24
   Group Size 24
   Group Composition 25
   Task Instructions 25
   Breakout Room/Area Assignments 26
   Equipment and Supplies 26

TOOLS 27

Visual Aids 27
   Common Mistakes When Using Visuals 28
   Special Hints for Using Flipcharts 31
   Special Hints for Using Chalkboards 33
   Special Hints for Using Whiteboards 33
   Special Hints for Using Overhead Projectors 34
   Special Hints for Using 35-mm Slide Projectors 35

Audio-Visual Aids 36
   Common Mistakes When Using Audio-Visuals 36
   Special Hints for Using Films and Videotapes 38
   Special Hints for Using 35-mm Slide/Tape 39

Table of Contents

SEASONINGS 41
    Personal Style and Approach 41
        Caring 41
        Enthusiasm 42
        Humor 43
        Listening 43
    Subject Matter Experts 44
        For Out-of-Class Assignments 44
        During the Class Session 45
        In Round-Table Discussions 46
        For Guest Presentations 46

CONTROLS 49
    Before Class Starts 49
        Room Setup 50
        Equipment and Supplies 50
    At the Start of Class 51
        Set the Stage 51
        Start on Time 51
        Clarify Expectations 51
    During the Class 52
        Respect 52
        Interest 53
        Checking on Results 54
        "Problem" Participants 54
    At the End of Class 58
    A Final Note 58

Table of Contents

RECIPES 59
  Using a Recipe 59
  Introducing Topics 61
    New Information 61
    Bridging from Previous Session or Assignment 61
    Building on Existing Knowledge/Experience 62
  Lecture 63
    Lecturette 63
    Participative Lecture 64
  Discussions, Course-Leader Led 66
    Information-Gathering 67
    Experience-Sharing 68
    Case Study 69
  Discussions, Small-Group 70
    Information-Gathering/Experience-Sharing 71
    Application 72
  Experiential 73
    Role-Play 74
    Behavior-Modeling 75
    Interviewing 76
    Games and Simulations 78
  Individual Learning Experiences 80
    Interviewing 80
    Interactive Video 81
    Personal Computer 82
    Personal Logbook/Journal 83

A FINAL WORD OF ENCOURAGEMENT 85

HOW AM I DOING? 87

Words of Encouragement

For those of you who haven't had the opportunity to experience leading a course, a few words on the benefits of the course leader's role might be helpful.

Obviously, the position of course leader brings with it an increase in visibility — certainly within your organization and often beyond. Leadership roles like this are associated with enhancing careers, especially when these roles are associated with achieving "real-world" results and are recognized as making a contribution to the bottom line of the organization.

On a more personal level are the skills you can refine in learning situations — specifically, communication techniques that have application outside the classroom in any leadership position. Those of you with some coaching or teaching experience know the personal rewards and gratification that result from helping people learn. Those of you without this "firsthand" knowledge are in for an enjoyable discovery.

The purpose of this book is to provide you with some basic information on being an effective course leader. We're not getting into course or lesson plan design because you'll be working with materials that have already been designed and are currently in use. Your primary job will be to *help the participants learn.* Although you probably have technical expertise in the subject you are leading, you are not expected to be "the expert" — the expertise is built into the materials and design of the course. Your task is to help the participants get all they can from the course materials whether in the form of interactive videodisk, readings, videotapes, personal computer simulations or classroom activities. An important part of this task is to help the participants build the bridge for application to their jobs. Learning that stays in the classroom is the same as not having learned at all. A good course leader will use all available resources including the participants themselves. The knowledge and experience that already exists within the group, knowledge of issues relevant to the organization or location, coupled with new knowledge, help the group tailor the course material for specific application.

The cookbook format was chosen deliberately because an effective course leader is like a "master chef." The master chef starts with the basics — the tools of the trade and how to select and use them — the ingredients and how to select, prepare, and measure them — mixing the ingredients to develop specific flavors and textures and avoiding unwanted flavors and textures — taking a basic recipe and through the use of seasonings, both subtle and strong, inventing exciting new dishes — creating menus to fit the occasion by planning a sequence of dishes that attracts the eye and delights the palate. The course leader can accomplish much the same thing in the classroom. The tools, ingredients, seasonings and spices certainly are different, but how they are used, combined and added to basic recipes is very much the same. So read ahead, feast your eyes on the potpourri of methods, ingredients, seasonings and recipes. Think about the "dishes" you want to serve in your sessions and how you can create learning experiences that range from "picnics" to "banquets."

Enjoy!

Richard D. Colvin
The Learning Experience
Yorktown Heights, NY

METHODS

Methods

One of the first things the chef has to consider after selecting the dish to be prepared is how it is to be cooked. There are a number of cooking methods, each designed to produce a certain result. At the simplest — boiling an egg. At a more complex level, preparing a casserole by sauteing some ingredients, adding them to other ingredients in the casserole dish, placing it in the oven and baking it, and, finally, adding a topping and placing the dish under the broiler to let the topping brown or melt. The chef not only has to know how to use the methods individually, but has to know how to combine them to get superior results.

The same is true of the course leader. There are a number of basic methods for helping people learn. Each is designed to achieve a certain result. The *good* course leader is able to use each method successfully — the *expert* course leader can combine them creatively to produce superior results. As you go through the basic methods which follow, think about combinations which will provide your participants with a superior learning experience.

Lecture

Lecture is the traditional teaching technique we've all experienced in our formal educations and probably could be thought of as the **basic recipe** of the chef. It can provide a large number of "dishes," depending on the ingredients used and the chef's skill in preparing and combining them.

This is the method most commonly used when you have knowledge or information the participants do not have. The flow of information is from you, or the materials, to them. But, while it is probably the easiest to prepare (you are "the expert") and enables you to cover a lot of information in a relatively short time, like the basic recipe, it has some definite shortcomings. The basic recipe tends to be bland, tasteless and zestless — the typical lecture? Think back to when you attended a course taught by the traditional lecture method — think about what it was like — what were some of the thoughts, feelings and reactions you had at that time?

If you are like most people, the majority of your reactions were: "boring"; "I missed an important point early in the lecture and became totally lost"; "I had no way to check my understanding and became frustrated"; "The lecturer was interesting, but I didn't learn a heck of a lot"; etc.

Lecturing consists primarily of covering the material. The lecturer seldom checks understanding and seldom deviates from the prepared notes — the students are "empty vessels waiting to be filled from the fount of the teacher's knowledge." This is not to say that lecture should not be used. It has a very valuable place in the learning experience provided it is used wisely. Here are some techniques to help you use the lecture method more effectively:

Keep It Short — Easy to say but not always easy to do, especially when you really are the subject matter expert. The short lecture, or **Lecturette**, is a useful way of introducing new topics, ideas or materials. Typically, it takes less than five minutes to establish the rationale for the topic and to briefly describe it. From that point on, the participants should be involved in the process.

Keep It Simple — Choose your words carefully — build on what the participants already know — relate to their experience. Be careful using jargon. If you have to use technical terms, define them as you go. Watch the language level — don't use words that insult the participants' intelligence or go over their heads. Talk conversationally just as you would if you were explaining a concept or idea to a friend who is interested in what you do.

Keep It Visual — Make use of visual aids such as overhead projectors, flipcharts, chalk- or whiteboards. Use them to illustrate concepts and ideas. *But,* keep them *supportive,* not *overwhelming.* They should illustrate what you are saying and not be used as a script. You'll find more information on visuals in the chapter on **Tools.**

Make It Participative — Lecture *does not* have to be one-way. Sure, you have knowledge and information the participants don't have and your job is to help them. The unique feature of the **Participative Lecture** approach is the use of *questions* to help people learn. Questions are used to have your participants make learning points for you, to help them, and you, test their understanding, to get them to give examples of application, to lead them through a chain of reasoning and so forth. The task you have is to look at your material and design questions to help you teach it. A typical sequence might be a few minutes of lecturette — several questions to the group to test for understanding or to get examples of application — re-teaching as needed — more lecturette — more questions, etc. You'll find detailed information on using questions in the chapter on **Ingredients.**

Discussion

The discussion method is a more advanced recipe since it requires the use of assistant chefs (the participants) under the guidance of the head chef (the course leader). The assistant chefs bring their knowledge, experience and skills to bear on the various tasks required to provide, prepare, mix and marry the recipe's ingredients and, as does the head chef, the course leader functions as an overseer, coach, stimulator, facilitator and guide.

All participants in a class have some knowledge and background related to the subject. The discussion method helps you take advantage of that and enables you to help them teach themselves. Many "A-Ha's" are created through this method — a concept expressed from several viewpoints may give someone new insight or a new approach — participants find that other people are having the same problems and may find someone who has a solution. By thinking, and talking it through, they can even convince themselves whereas they might be skeptical if you told them the same thing.

There are several variations of the discussion recipe, and the one you use depends on the outcome you want.

INFORMATION-GATHERING — This variation is very useful for determining what the participants already know about the topic; for getting involvement in a nonthreatening way; and, for getting everyone to think. For example, if you are leading a course in manufacturing measurements, and want to show the variety of measurements being used locally, you could ask the question (an essential ingredient), "What are some of the manufacturing measurements used in your unit?" Get answers from various members of the group and list them on a flipchart or chalkboard, then use them as a springboard for discussion as to their value and use. This type of question does several things for you. First, it eliminates the need to *tell* the participants what the various measurements are. Second, it gives you a good idea of the extent of *their* knowledge. And, third, it gets people involved. You should have a good idea of what answers you should be getting and, if any important ones aren't brought out, the participants either don't know or don't recognize them, you can get the answers simply by saying ... "Let me contribute one," or, "How about ...?" Thus, you can provide needed input without sounding as if you are lecturing. The information flow in this kind of discussion would look something like this:

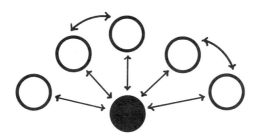

EXPERIENCE-SHARING — This variation enables participants to explore one another's attitudes; arrive at solutions to problems; share knowledge, experiences and insights; and, again, get people involved. As with the **Information-Gathering** discussion, *you* have to determine the learning outcome — that is, you go in knowing what you want the participants to learn. The main part of your job is to design questions to keep them on track. If the discussion will extend over a series or sequence of issues, you need to prepare starting questions for each issue. An example of this might be, "Suppose you ...(pose a hypothetical issue)..., what would you do about it?" Ask the question to the group and let them bat it around for a while, stimulating them as appropriate with questions or "what ifs."

CASE STUDY — This is a variation on a variation. It is a combination of the **Information-Gathering** and **Experience-Sharing** discussions. In this instance, the **Case Study** serves as the vehicle for discussion. Participants share their understanding of the facts, analyze and review actions described in the case, and draw conclusions from the case. This variation can be used with the whole group with the course leader facilitating, but it is best suited for small group or "buzz" group exercises.

In both the **Experience-Sharing** and **Case Study** variations, the information flow is primarily among the group members and would look something like this:

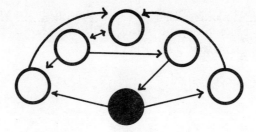

SETTING THE CLIMATE — Among the factors the chef has to take into consideration when using or creating a recipe are: **Temperature** — do things need to be kept cold as in making pastry dough or do some ingredients need to be melted before they can be used? **Moisture** — which ingredients are to be mixed dry and when are liquids to be added? **Condition** — are the vegetables to be crisp or limp, how finely should they be chopped? In effect, the chef is creating a climate for the dish being created.

The course leader, too, has to create a climate for discussion. Since it is psychological, rather than environmental, it is essential that it be an *open* climate — one that stimulates discussion. This is done through the use of open-ended questions and being receptive to contributions from members of the class. The use of too many controlling words, questions or sentences *closes* the climate. Benjamin Franklin accurately described the need to create an open and accepting climate:

> "If you state an opinion to me in a dogmatic manner, which is in direct opposition to my thought and you imply no room to negotiate, then I must conclude, in order to protect my own self-esteem, that you are wrong and will immediately undertake to prove you wrong ... On the other hand, if you state your opinion as a hypothesis with evidence of a willingness to *discuss* and *explore*, I will most likely undertake to prove you correct."

Being able to lead a stimulating and interesting discussion in an open climate is a special skill, but the skill can be learned. Some basic guidelines for successful discussions are:

Provide Background — Provide background for the discussion. It can be a case study, a report, a current topic, a problem that has been experienced in the shop or whatever is appropriate to the learning objective. After presenting the background, open the discussion with a question that allows many "right" answers.

Wait — Now comes the first test — waiting for someone to answer. You may feel nervous, impatient or even uncomfortable with the silence. *But, wait it out!* If the question is thought-provoking, you can't expect to get instant answers. In fact, if you do get instant answers, that's a sign that little thinking was required or done. Of course, if the silence goes on too long, you will probably have to rephrase your question. Watch the group. Sometimes body language and facial expressions will indicate that they did not understand your question.

Acknowledge Contributions — As the discussion starts, acknowledge contributions with a nod of the head, a brief comment such as, "That's a good thought," or, "I see," or even a grunt or, "Uh huh." At this stage remain neutral, don't agree or disagree with what is being said. All you're doing right now is acknowledging the contribution. There will be temptation to say something like, "That's right," or, "Yeah, that's what I had in mind." You need to be careful of this because it might imply to the class that you are looking for the "right" answer and are steering the discussion the way *you* want it to go. Let the questions do the steering.

Record Contributions — As the discussion progresses, and if you are in the information-gathering mode, write their answers on the flipchart or chalk- or whiteboard. This way you can capture the contributions and expand on them as appropriate. They serve as a record of what is being said and the act of writing them provides the individual with a feeling of recognition. And, when it's time to close out the discussion, you can use them as a summary.

Keep Control — In a well-run kitchen things usually go smoothly under the direction of the chef. However, there are times, particularly during the stress of preparing a large number of meals simultaneously, when things start falling apart and the chef is ready to start screaming, ranting and raving. The professional chef will avoid that trap and will quickly restore control.

In the classroom it is sometimes difficult to keep participants on the main subject, especially when they are engaged in a spirited discussion. But keeping control is an important part of your job. As you maintain order and direction, you gain the respect of the group. Often this can be done with a simple comment such as, "This has been an interesting detour, but we need to get back to the subject," and then restate the objective. Sometimes discussion begins with two participants, becomes hot and heavy, and the rest of the class is excluded. When this happens the other participants relax, become spectators and cease to contribute. One way to break this up is to say, "How about that idea, anyone else have any opinions on it?" This can get the others involved without embarrassing the two who started the discussion.

Experiential

The training a chef goes through is rigorous, to say the least. A lot of time is spent cracking the books and being in class, but the real learning goes on in the kitchen where the "book learning" is put to use. It is an apprenticeship method. The entry-level chef usually starts out peeling vegetables and doing other mundane tasks. As time passes and experience builds, he or she is allowed to prepare standard, simple dishes. Beginning chefs make a lot of mistakes, are criticized for them, but learn from them. They are completely immersed in an *experiential* environment.

This method produces learning by having participants *experience* the very concepts you want to teach, rather than merely studying or talking about them or analyzing them as in case studies. However, they learn not so much from what they *do*, but from what *happens to them while they do it*. They may experience anger, frustration, intimidation or excitement. They may react by attacking, resisting, withdrawing or fleeing. They may suffer the consequences of overlooking a key principle or experience the pleasure of applying a process successfully. The task is to help them analyze the experience and relate it to the learning objectives.

The most common ways of providing experiential learning are through **Role-Play, Games, Simulations, Creating "A-Ha's," Laboratories, Interactive Personal Computer** and **Interactive Video.** Each of these is covered in more detail below.

ROLE-PLAY — Part of the training a chef gets is in the dining room, waiting on tables or serving as bus boy or bus girl. These duties are not part of the chef's job but he or she needs to know what goes on at that end of the business. In effect, this experience is a form of role-play. That is, assuming a role not normally yours and trying to function effectively in it. Role-play provides the opportunity to try out new techniques and processes in a simulated situation.

Many people look at role-play as "play-acting" and try to carry out their parts as actors. This is unfortunate because role-play is really an opportunity to "do it live." At times scripts may be provided but, for the most part, only the job functions (i.e., a manager and an engineer who is a direct report), the stances to be taken (i.e., manager, you are very annoyed; employee, you are defensive), and sometimes, the situation (i.e., manager, you're trying to correct the employee's habit of tardiness; employee, you have to take your child to a special school every morning) are suggested.

Some of the purposes of role-play are to provide an opportunity to practice using a new process or skill, to illustrate what happens when something goes right (or wrong), or to serve as a vehicle for analysis. To make the role-play more meaningful, the participants can be asked to use a situation that actually happened on the job or one they plan to do soon and would like to try out in class. This is particularly valuable in *behavior-modeling* situations. Practice through role-play has a much greater impact when the situations used are real world.

GAMES — These are experiences ranging from board games where pieces are moved, based on decisions made in response to posed situations, to interpersonal activities designed to illustrate what happens when groups or individuals operate in a competitive environment. While most games are designed to be played in small groups which compete with one another, some games are played by individuals using the personal computer and associated software. Games help the learning process by making the scoring dependent on how well the principles, techniques, functions, etc., being taught are applied. If competition is a factor, it could be on an individual level among members of a small group or on a group level between small groups. This provides an additional opportunity to explore how people work together in a competitive climate.

SIMULATIONS — These are activities which have many of the same characteristics as games, such as decision-making, scoring, competition, etc., but are much more realistic. They try to replicate the actual conditions being described, but permit errors without disastrous consequences. For example, airline pilots spend many hours in simulators before they get into real cockpits and fly planes. The simulation is so real they think they *are* flying the plane. With a simulation, it is possible to set up many conditions that *could* happen to give the individuals practice in handling them. If mistakes are made, no one is hurt.

Classroom simulations are usually not as elaborate as those used to train pilots. Many of them are pencil-and-paper exercises. Situations reflecting actual conditions are set up. Participants apply what they are learning to the situations, make decisions, implement plans and see results. In a course in project management, a simulation is used which requires the teams to apply the planning and project-management techniques they are learning to create an assembly line and operate it to assemble a model engine. Throughout the simulation, participants act as a project team dealing with the same conditions a real project team is subjected to. They follow all the required procedures and make the necessary decisions in response to conditions as they occur during the course of the simulation.

When using **Games** and **Simulations,** make sure the participants understand the purpose of the exercise, the roles assigned, rules to follow and results required.

CREATING "A-HA's" — The "A-Ha" is a valuable learning experience because it literally and figuratively lights the "lamp of learning" (often depicted as the illuminated light bulb over someone's head). Most "A-Ha's" occur in the natural course of events — someone has difficulty comprehending a concept or is struggling with a sticky problem and, all of a sudden, someone says something, or the individual sees something that contains the missing piece, and all the pieces fall into place and, "A-Ha, there's the answer!"

As a course leader, you can create "A-Ha's" for your participants. This is usually done through setups where, on the surface, you seem to be doing or saying one thing, but, underneath, you are accomplishing something else. Here are some ways this can be done:

Deliberate "Failure" Experience — Present participants with a problem or situation, have them work on it using their present skills/knowledge, *knowing they won't succeed*. After they "bomb," you demonstrate the new knowledge/skill and resolve the situation or problem in short order. Your objective? To get people to think or say, "Hey, maybe there *is* something here I can use. *My* technique didn't work."

Controversial Stand — Another type of setup is when you deliberately take a controversial stand. If the subject is performance appraisal and the point you're trying to make is that it is difficult to defend a low rating on a personality trait such as attitude and a class member disagrees with you, you can play the role of the low-rated employee ... "What do you mean only a two on attitude? My attitude is as good as anyone else's around here." And every time the participant tries to defend the rating, jump on him and force him into a corner.

The Garden Path — Another way to create an "A-Ha" is through a carefully designed line of questions to lead the participants down the desired path of reasoning and let *them* draw the conclusion you want.

About the only limiting factor in creating "A-Ha's" is your imagination and comfort level for risk-taking.

LABORATORIES — These are job-oriented group activities that require the application of what has been learned. It may be using videotape equipment to record practice interviews, or it may be the group working together to solve an operations problem or it may be preparing a team presentation on some aspect of research they've done. In a sense, the laboratory is an extension of the classroom but without course-leader involvement.

The effective chef uses state-of-the-art tools and methods such as food processors and microwave ovens for appropriate applications. The effective course leader also uses state-of-the-art tools and methods. Among these are the interactive personal computer and interactive video. These are experiential in that they are very effective for simulations.

INTERACTIVE PERSONAL COMPUTER — The personal computer is often used to simulate the operation of a business. Information is supplied, decisions are made and results are shown, usually on a spreadsheet. They are particularly valuable for "what-if" applications where variable parameters can be changed and their effects seen immediately.

INTERACTIVE VIDEO — The interactive video is available in two forms: videotape and videodisk. Interactive video also simulates business conditions but usually emphasizes interpersonal rather than financial aspects. In its simplest form, interactive video shows either an instructor or a vignette, asks a question (or questions), and the participant answers via the keyboard. The answer is compared to the right answer and the participant gets feedback on accuracy. In the more advanced forms, the participant can simulate an actual operation, access more information or specific details using a light pen or touch screen, and can be channeled along specific paths of reasoning through the branching capabilities. The videotape format is a less expensive system but videodisk, through its random-access nature, is much faster and more flexible. As good courseware becomes available, these tools are getting more and more use.

While both the interactive personal computer and interactive video can be used for small-group activities, they are best suited for individual learning.

INGREDIENTS

Ingredients

One of the things that differentiates a chef from a cook is the selection and preparation of the ingredients that go into a dish. This ranges from the recipe itself (there are many variations on a theme), through the quality of the ingredients and their preparation, to the final mixing, combining and cooking. A cook may take short cuts, save money through inferior ingredients, skip some preparation steps and kind of throw things together. The results may be edible, but not many people would ask for seconds. The chef, on the other hand, selects the appropriate version of the recipe, obtains quality ingredients, takes pains with their preparation and blends them with loving care. The result? A meal which never overfills and always has people coming back for more.

The same holds true for the successful course leader. Your ingredients are different but their selection, preparation and blending are just as critical. Let's look at some of the major ingredients you'll probably be working with.

Lesson Plan

If you are a member of the audience for whom this book was written, you will be using lesson plans that have already been developed (just as the chef uses a recipe from a cookbook). Most course leader guides and lesson plans are well-designed to ease the burden of the course leader, but this doesn't mean that you can just pick up the guide on the day of the class and use it effectively. Try that and watch your souffle fall flat on its pan! Your task is twofold: First, to become thoroughly familiar with the lesson plan for each session you're going to lead — the flow of activities, the visuals being used, the exercises. Second, *make it you*. Avoid the trap of using it as a script. Study the learning objectives, understand the rationale behind each activity, and put them in your own words. Look for appropriate places to ask questions, to get discussions going, to test for understanding, and mark them in the lesson plan. Use the timing shown as a guide — not as gospel. Be flexible. If a discussion is taking longer than anticipated, but it's fruitful, look ahead to see which other activity could be condensed to make up for it.

Don't become lesson-plan bound. Sometimes the group goes off on a tangent, usually because they think it's important. If it is important and they're getting something useful from it, let it go on for a few minutes. Keep listening to what they're saying and looking for a hook to get you back to the topic ... then you can say something like, "That's an interesting point. See how it fits in with (your topic)." Sometimes you can't find a hook so just say, "This has been an interesting discussion, but we're getting away from our topic. Let's get back on course." Most of the time this will bring the class right back.

Course Leader's Knowledge

This is an essential ingredient of most recipes for successful learning experiences, but one which must be used with care. Like many spices and herbs, its flavor can be overpowering. Most of the time the effective course leader uses just enough to provide a hint of flavor. There will be times when you'll have knowledge and information your participants don't have and you'll have to increase the quantity of this ingredient. But the flavor can be moderated by the way you present it. Garlic in its raw form can be overpowering but, when baked, can provide a delicious taste treat. If you use traditional **Lecture** to get your points across, it may be overpowering; if you use **Participative Lecture**, it can be very palatable. You also have to use your knowledge and experience to guide the session. You can use your knowledge to help you test for understanding and to develop questions that get participants to bring out important points. You can use your knowledge to expand on ideas or to clarify areas of confusion. Use your knowledge and experience, but always with the thought, "What will happen to my 'dish' if there is too much of this ingredient?"

Participants' Knowledge and Experience

Some ingredients in a recipe or meal are never overpowering. They add to the flavor and zest of the dish and you can't really overuse them. The knowledge and experience of your participants is just such an ingredient. It doesn't matter if they are entry-level or old hands, they all have knowledge and backgrounds that can be built upon. The successful course leader *looks* for ways to use this ingredient. It's almost like bread dough. Give it the proper climate and the yeast in it grows and causes the dough to rise. Punch it down, knead it, pummel it, roll it out, put it back into the bowl and it rises again. Soon you have many times the quantity you started with. You can form it into different shapes and sizes, and you can add special flavorings or coloring. In fact, it can be a work of art! Learn to use this versatile ingredient. It will become one of your favorites.

Questioning

The questioning technique is by far the single most important ingredient for the effective course leader. It is akin to the whole array of ingredients the chef uses; in addition to a few general-purpose ingredients, there are many specialized ones. The untrained cook may not recognize the differences, but the experienced chef picks the right one for the job.

Most texts and articles on using questions as a teaching tool deal with them in terms such as "open-ended," "closed-ended," "factual," "overhead," "relay," etc., to describe their use and you have to try to remember, "When do I use an open-ended question as opposed to an overhead question?" Instead, let's look at questions in terms of "What do I want to accomplish?"

There are two main categories of questions that you'll use throughout your course-leading experience: **Content-Specific** and **Generic**.

Content-Specific Questions — These deal with the actual subject matter. They relate to the specific points, ideas, concepts, data and information being taught. Some examples:

- "What are the key problems facing the manager in the case we just read?"
- "Give me an example of where this process can be used in your job."
- "Name two key ingredients of motivation."

Content-specific questions are excellent tools to:

- Identify details
- Get at causes or facts
- Reinforce specific learning points
- Call attention to another phase of the problem
- Test for understanding
- Find out what the participants already know about the topic.

Generic Questions — These are questions that can be used with any topic. They usually deal with exploring participants' attitudes, feelings and opinions. Some examples are:

- "Why do you say that?"
- "Give me an example."
- "Expand on that."

- "In what way?"
- "What's your opinion on that, (name)?"

Generic questions are excellent tools to:
- Get involvement
- Stimulate discussion
- Test an individual's reasoning — *comprehension — scope*
- Uncover sources of information
- Change group thinking.

Within each category, there are questions for specific uses. Let's look at some of the more common uses.

TO INTRODUCE TOPICS — The typical way of introducing new topics is the **Lecture** or **Lecturette.** That is, you just say, … "Now, we're going to look at …" Questions can be a very effective way of introducing new topics, particularly if you want to get immediate involvement and build on participants' prior knowledge and/or experience. One way of doing this is to ask a hypothetical question. For example, if you wanted to move into the topic of quality-control measurements, you might ask, "Let's say you're producing (product name). How do you know how well the finished product is meeting customer specifications?" This would probably get answers such as, "Check them against the QC specs"… or "Quality Control will tell us." You can then follow up with the question, "What kinds of things do the QC people look for?" or any other question which would help you introduce specific quality measurements. Sure, you can simply say, "Okay, now we're going to look at quality control measurements and how they help us produce quality products"… but then you lose the opportunity of immediate involvement and heightening of the participants' interest level. *Good point*

In your preparation for course leading, develop the habit of looking at your course material and lesson plan and developing questions to help you get into a new topic.

This has the added benefit of enabling you to tailor your approach to the specific conditions and/or practices of your organization.

TO GET EXAMPLES/EXPERIENCES — The best way to make learning relevant to the participants is to relate it to their backgrounds by getting them to give examples of application or lack of application and by getting them to share relevant experiences. There are several ways of doing this. One is to direct a question to a specific individual ... "Bob, what has been your experience with this?" Another, is to direct the question to the group ... "Who can give us an example of ...?" You also might want to bring out opinions ..."That's an interesting point, (to a participant's comment). Mike, what's your opinion on that?"

Examples are a powerful means of getting participants to see, understand and accept the need and relevance of what you're teaching. The examples need to be ones the participants can relate to so they should be taken from the participants' job situations. The best examples in terms of relevance, of course, are from the participants themselves. When you are preparing to lead your course, look for every opportunity to use examples and build on participant experience. Think about how you want to use these ingredients, then develop questions to bring them out and write them in your lesson plan.

TO GET MORE INFORMATION — There will be many times when you'll want to get your participants to expand on points being made. This can range from getting an individual to amplify on what he or she has said, to getting the group as a whole to explore the topic in greater detail. Again, the question is your key tool. Some questions you can ask are:

- "How do you know that?"
- "Build on that a little."
- "How would you go about doing that?"
- "What other things might be considered?"

20

- "Such as?"
- "How would that help?"

✓ **TO GET CLARIFICATION** — You can also use questions to get a person to clarify a stand that he or she has taken, particularly if it is counter to what you are trying to get across.
- "Why do you say that?"
- "What are some specific examples of …?"
- "What leads you to draw that conclusion?"
- "Assuming that is so, how does it explain …?"

✓ **TO FOLLOW UP** — When you are preparing to lead your course, always prepare follow-up questions to the main questions you plan to ask. Many times you'll get short or incomplete answers and you'll want to get expansion of the answer or want to probe the reasoning behind it. The more questions you have in your tool kit, the easier it will be to do this.

✓ **TO TEST UNDERSTANDING** — This is a vital ingredient of any learning experience. Just as the chef monitors progress by tasting, testing and observing *while the dish is being prepared* (because if he or she waited until it was done, it would be too late to make corrections), the course leader has to do the same. You can't wait until the end of the session or the course to test understanding. If participants fail the test, it's too late to reteach them. Testing has to be a continuous process. However, it should be unobstrusive and, if done correctly, the participants don't even know they are being tested. This is where your content-specific questions come into use. As you complete each learning point, ask several test-for-understanding questions. If the answers indicate that the participants have understood, summarize and move on to the next learning point; if the answers indicate a lack of understanding of all or some part, you can back up and clarify the point not grasped. And, since you are teaching through questioning anyway, it doesn't seem like a test.

In your preparation, identify points where you plan to test for understanding, develop some content-specific questions, and write them in your lesson plan.

TO TEST FOR APPLICATION — Understanding a concept or idea is only part of the equation; for learning to pay off, it has to be applied. Your questions can help your participants identify applications to their specific situations. These questions can be content-specific, generic or a combination of the two. The primary purpose of the question is to help people see that the new knowledge, skill or technique can be applied personally and get them to think about how to go about it. Some questions might be:

- "Tom, how do you see this fitting into your work?"
- "How would you go about implementing this process?"
- "What problems do you see in implementing it?"
- "What can you do to prevent these problems or at least minimize their effects?"

Again, in your preparation, look for opportunities to build in these questions.

Examples

These are like the illustrations in a cookbook ... they help the chef recognize various ingredients, preparation methods, tools to be used and what the completed dish should look like. They may be simple line drawings or full-color photographs. They may be humorous or they may be serious. Whatever they are, they serve a valuable purpose.

Examples in a classroom also serve a valuable purpose. They provide mental hooks on which the participants can hang new information. They help participants see applications of what they are learning and help them relate this learning to their jobs and lives. Through examples, the participants can bridge the gap between the abstract and reality; between "nice to know" and "need to apply." But, just as an illustration can contain so much detail that it's difficult to identify its important features, an example can also cause more confusion than clarification.

An example should communicate, help to make an abstract idea or concept come to life. It should make it easy to see the value of the idea and opportunities for application; to get it out of the realm of "sounds great in class, but ..." to "Hey, that really makes sense and I know just where I'll use it."

Examples should be brief, to the point, relevant and timely. As you go through your lesson plan, look for places to insert examples and, while you'll probably have to provide some, the best place to get them is from the participants themselves. "Give me an example of ..." carries more weight than "For example ...." Examples can also be a metaphor or an analogy, such as this book.

Demonstration

Demonstration is an important learning ingredient. Demonstrating means actually doing something. It takes participants from knowing What, Why and How on an intellectual level to pragmatic application. A good demonstration is one of the most powerful convincers there is. By virtue of demonstration they know, "By golly, it works!"

Demonstrations can be passive activities — such as viewing a film or videotape showing a process being applied — or watching the course leader or a fellow participant doing something. It can be a hands-on activity where each participant gets a chance to try it. Which you use depends on what you're trying to accomplish. There are some hidden traps in demonstrations. They take time and people often get caught up in the content and lose sight of the process being demonstrated. But, despite that, it is a powerful learning ingredient.

Small-Group Activities

The small-group activity is a major ingredient of an effective learning experience. It is a multi-purpose ingredient because it can be used for activities as diverse as problem-solving, case studies, role-playing, exploring situations, answering questions, developing ideas, applying techniques, managing projects and a host of other things. The small-group activity fosters involvement and the use of personal knowledge and experience and it gives people an opportunity to learn from each other as group members defend personal viewpoints and attempt to influence the viewpoints of their colleagues. As in any ingredient we use, effective preparation is a *must* if the activity is going to be successful. Among the things we need to consider are: group size and composition, where participants will work, instructions for what they're to do and the equipment and supplies they'll need. *Plus they get involved which in itself is often a breakthrough.*

GROUP SIZE — Group size is important — too few and you don't have enough; too many, and people get in each other's way. An absolute minimum (by definition) is three. A group of three is usable but really lacks enough people to form a critical mass. They are good in practice situations such as behavior-modeling or role-play where the third party can provide feedback to the two principles, but they're not very good for generating new ideas — just not enough heads. A group of seven or more gets unwieldy. Sometimes they break up into several factions or the more verbal members take over and the timid ones retreat to the sidelines. Many times there are just too many diverse opinions and they can't reach a consensus.

A good, workable size is four, five or six. There are enough to get cross-fertilization of ideas but not too many to get in the way. Your class size may be a determining factor in selecting group size. If you have only six participants, you are limited to two groups of three. If you have 18 participants, you can have three groups of six. While it's nice to have groups of the same size, it's not always possible. If you have 11 people, your choices are two groups of five and six, respectively, or two groups of four and one of three.

GROUP COMPOSITION — Composition is important, too. If you are looking for a broad perspective or viewpoint, a cross-functional group (representing different job functions) is good. If you want specific expertise to be brought to bear on a problem or situation, a group composed of people with that background would be appropriate. For the most part, however, you can get good results through a random group assignment. Often, your lesson plan will suggest how to structure your group.

TASK INSTRUCTIONS — The group has to have a clear understanding of what they are to do during the activity and the results they are to obtain. A useful way to do this is to give the instructions in writing as well as verbally. This way they have something to refer to during the activity when someone says, "What is it we're supposed to do?" The instructions should be brief and explicit, usually in outline form. They should detail the situation or problem to be worked on, describe the types of actions or techniques the group should apply and indicate what they should bring back as a result of their efforts. And, of course, the amount of time they have.

BREAKOUT ROOM/AREA ASSIGNMENTS — Small groups need a place to work. They should be able to sit comfortably, have a table to work around, a flipchart to use if a presentation to the class is to be the final product, and any other special equipment that might be needed. Where they work depends on what space is available. Many times separate breakout rooms are used; these provide a good degree of isolation and get the participants up on their feet to move to the room. Another option is to use a separate room large enough to accommodate all the groups with some degree of isolation, using screens if available, or placing a group in each corner of the room. And, if you want or need the groups to share their intermediate results, or have additional input to give them part-way through the activity, you can have them work in the classroom by moving their chairs together as groups. The noise level is much higher, but sometimes that stimulates the group process. It's a good idea to visit the groups periodically, particularly in the early stages of the activity. This will enable you to monitor their progress and make sure they understand the results expected. These visits should be unobtrusive and you should comment only if you see they didn't understand the instructions or if they ask you a question.

EQUIPMENT AND SUPPLIES — While most small-group activities require no more than a flipchart easel, pad and marking pens, there may be some activities requiring equipment as elaborate as a complete videotape setup (camera, tape deck, monitor, lights, microphone) or a personal computer workstation or as simple as parts for a game, puzzle or product to be assembled. Part of your job is to make sure that all required equipment, supplies and parts are available, set up and in working order. Also, if possible, have back-up equipment and spare pieces available in the event something breaks down or is missing.

TOOLS

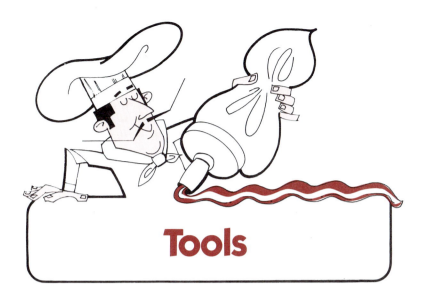

Tools

The chef has a wide variety of tools available — ranging from pots and pans, through utensils such as knives, forks and spoons, to electrical appliances such as mixers, blenders and food processors. In each category are tools for specialized applications: pots and pans for stove-top cooking, oven cooking, and microwave-oven cooking; knives for cutting, chopping, paring, boning, slicing; long and short forks as well as blending forks; and so on.

These tools not only have to be available, the chef has to know which ones to use and how to use them. Try boning a roast with a cleaver and see what happens. In acquiring these tools, the effective chef also considers quality ... poor-quality tools usually give poor-quality results.

The course leader, too, has many tools available for creating learning experiences. Detailing them all probably would take an encyclopedia, but there are some tools of particular value in the classroom.

Visual Aids

Experience has shown that people learn more through their eyes than their ears and that understanding is quicker when illustration replaces words. Some of the most effective advertisements have few written words. In Japan, restaurant businesses carry this concept a step further — they use lifelike models of their dishes in addition to written menus. This makes a lot of sense; you really can't tell what an entree will be like just from its description in the menu. (By the way, visual menu model-making has become an art and big business in Japan.) Some restaurants here may show you a sample of a special dish, but that practice is rare.

The same concept holds true in the classroom. The more of the participants' senses we can engage, the quicker and deeper the understanding. Part of your preparation should be reading your lesson plan and identifying places in which you can use visual as well as verbal means to get the message across and, if possible, think in terms of pictures, diagrams and symbols in place of words. Design them using your mind's eye, get them down on paper to see what they'll look like and, if convenient, have them prepared and ready to use ahead of time. The most commonly used visual aids are the flipchart, chalkboard, whiteboard and overhead projector. First we'll look at some common mistakes made in using visuals, then some special hints for each.

Common Mistakes When Using Visuals

Blocking with your body: It is difficult to write on a flipchart pad, chalkboard, whiteboard or overhead projector transparency without blocking someone's view, usually on your right when using flipchart and the boards and on your left when using the overhead projector.
To overcome this, write quickly; then step back.

Illegible writing or printing: In the give-and-take of classroom discussion we feel pressured to write quickly and, as a result, to scribble and abbreviate.
To overcome this, take your time. If you're getting input from a participant, listen first, then write. If the input is lengthy, listen, capture the essential point(s), then write them, remembering to check with the participant ... "Does that capture what you said?"

Writing too small: There are a couple of things that could make you write too small. First, when you are at the flipchart or board, small letters look okay — *you* have no trouble reading them. Second, you may be using lined flipchart paper, in which case there is a strong temptation to fit the letters between adjacent lines. The problem is, these are usually one inch apart and you end up with one-inch letters.

To overcome this, write for the person sitting farthest from you. If you are using lined paper, fit your letters between every other line — that will give you two-inch letters.

Talking to the board: There is a psychological phenomenon all course leaders experience at the easel or board — Fear of Silence. This fear is so strong that many course leaders continue talking as they are writing. In effect, they are talking to the board, not to the class.

To overcome this, do two things. First, realize that the silence is more apparent to you than to the participants — they are usually copying what you are writing and don't notice the silence. Second, you can say it to them first, then write it, then step back and repeat what you wrote. This gives them three opportunities to capture your point, and all your talking is to the class.

Too much content: Some course leaders feel the need to show as much information as possible, usually in the form of words. As a result, the writing is too small to be read from the back of the room; participants write furiously to capture it all or say, "The heck with it," and don't write anything, and the learning point is lost in the mass of words.

To overcome this, keep words to a minimum. Wherever possible, use pictures, illustrations, diagrams, graphs, to get the point across. Remember, visual images are powerful learning tools.

Reading from the visual: This is particularly common when using prepared charts or transparencies. They usually contain a lot of points in outline form and the course leader reads them aloud, word for word. The unintended implication is that the participants don't know how to read!

To overcome this, keep the information brief and either let the visual support what you are saying, or verbally expand on what they are seeing. If you verbally expand, paraphrase rather than read word for word.

Talking while they are reading: Another common mistake with prepared visuals. A page or transparency may have five or six points in outline form and you want to expand on each one, in turn. But, while you are talking about point number one, they are reading points four, five and six. Another psychological phenomenon: When people are reading and copying from your visuals, they tend to stop listening to what you're saying.

To overcome this, mask what you don't want them to read in advance. With a flipchart, chalk or whiteboard, tape paper strips over each point and remove them as you get to them. With an overhead transparency, use a piece of paper to cover the points you don't want visible and slide it down to uncover these points when you are ready for them. (By the way, the paper works best when placed *under* the transparency — it won't get blown off by a stray breeze or accidentally moved.)

Inappropriate use of color: While color can add to the impact of a visual, some course leaders use it with wild abandon ..."It'll jazz it up, make it look pretty," etc. As a result, it defeats the purpose of the visual. Color by itself means nothing and can actually create confusion.

To overcome this, plan your use of color in advance. When you are designing your visuals, use color to highlight key words or to show relationships (all inputs to a workstation in blue, all outputs in green and all intermediate processes in brown) and, to a much lesser degree, to provide some variety and a change of pace.

Which colors we use is a critical decision, particularly in terms of visibility. Some colors are easier to see from a distance than are others. On flipcharts and whiteboards, stay with the basic black, blue, green, brown, purple. Avoid yellow, pink, light orange or any other "invisible" color. Minimize the use of red. Red ink on a white background is very difficult to read from a distance. Chalkboards have their own problems, depending on the background color. Try out different colors of chalk to see which give the best visibility. On overhead projectors, all but the light shades will probably work but, again, it depends on the background color of the acetate itself.

Confusing diagrams: Diagrams showing relationships, process steps, or some kind of flow or sequence can be very complex and, if presented to the group in their completed form, may cause confusion. People tend to try to mentally reconstruct them to understand the chain of reasoning behind them.

To overcome this, build the diagrams as you explain what's happening. On a flipchart, chalk or whiteboard, you can draw them as you go. On an overhead transparency, you can either draw them as you go or use a series of overlays and add each one as you talk about it.

Special Hints for Using FLIPCHARTS:

- Always check your paper pad to make sure you have enough for the session and no one else has used sheets inside and left them there.

- Be sure the easel legs are locked into place and that the easel is steady and the paper pad is securely fastened.

- Use marking pens with broad, chisel tips rather than pointed tips — broad lines are easier to see. Always check the pens before class and discard the ones that seem to be going dry — continuing to use them is false economy. Water-based ink is preferable to oil-based — it won't bleed through to the next page and it will generally wash out of your clothes. If using oil-based marking pens, replace the cap as soon as you stop writing — they dry out fast and once dried out are unusable.

- If you're going to do a lot of work using the easel, have at least two, maybe three. This way, as you complete a page on one, you can carry the idea over to the next one without losing your train of thought. Also, the points already made remain visible, providing continuity.

- When you are finished with a topic and are ready to move on the the next topic, clear the boards! Flip over to a fresh sheet on each easel. If you want to keep some of the previous information visible for a time, tear the sheet off and tape or pin it to the wall. Leaving it visible on the easel just confuses people.

- Position the easels so that everybody can easily see them. If you are using a narrow room with a U-shaped table arrangement and two or three easels, the people along the legs of the "U" may have difficulty seeing the right or left easel. If necessary, move them as you use them.

- If you want to get extra involvement, appoint one of your participants to write on the easel during class discussions. This frees you to concentrate on facilitating the discussion.

- If you want to prepare your charts in advance, but want it to appear as if you're doing it in class, put your notes on the page in pencil. You can even put diagrams on that way and just trace over the lines with your marking pen.

Remember to use a light touch with the pencil, so it won't be visible to the participants, especially those closest to the easel.

Special Hints for Using CHALKBOARDS:

- Check out the board before class, making sure it is erased and washed.

- Check out your chalk supply. Make sure you have enough chalk and the colors you plan to use.

- Make sure the erasers are clean. Chalk-covered erasers just smear the board.

- When erasing, do a thorough job. Some authorities say an up-and-down motion is better than side-to-side. Experiment for yourself to find the best way for you.

- Use chalkboard only for items of a temporary nature. If you want to keep something visible throughout the session, use flipchart paper and hang it on the wall.

- Be careful if you tape anything to the chalkboard surface — it might leave a sticky residue that would be hard to write over or to clean.

Special Hints for Using WHITEBOARDS:

- A whiteboard is a high-tech chalkboard that uses marking pens rather than chalk. It can be in easel form or mounted on the wall. Most of the comments related to the use of flipcharts and chalkboards apply to whiteboards.

- **Major Caution** — Use only pens designed for whiteboards! Pens normally used with flipcharts are indelible on whiteboards. If you have both flipcharts and whiteboards in the room, it is a good practice to use only markers made for whiteboards. Do not allow regular flipchart markers in the classroom!

Special Hints for Using
OVERHEAD PROJECTORS:

- Check out the projector before class to see that it works and make sure you have a spare projection bulb. Some models have the spare bulb built in — all you do is turn a knob to move it into place. Check it out! The last person to use the projector may have done this and not replaced the defective bulb.

- Place the projector on a low table or firm chair seat so the arm carrying the projection lens does not block the view of participants. Make sure it is focused. Walk to the rear of the room to make sure the projected image is clear and legible.

- Tilt the top of the projection screen forward to minimize or avoid the "keystone" effect.

- Prepare your transparencies well in advance of the class. Your leader guide will probably contain reproducible masters you can use.

- Have your transparencies arranged in the proper sequence of use and placed at the side of the projector out of the air stream from the cooling fan.

- Use cardboard or plastic frames for your transparencies. They are easier to handle and you can write notes on them to help you explain what's on each transparency.

- When pointing out items on the transparency to the class, either stand at the side of the screen and use a pointer (face the group as you do this) or sit down next to the projector, facing the class, and use a small pointer (a transparent swizzle stick with a point is perfect). Under no circumstances stand at the projector to do this. You are certain to block someone's view or the projected image.

- Turn the lamp off when changing transparencies. This eliminates the bright light on the screen between transparencies.

- If you want to reveal a bit of information at a time, place a piece of paper *under* the transparency and slide it down as you get to each bit of data.

- If you're going to write on the transparency while it is being projected, use the special transparency marking pens available. Make sure they work okay before class starts. Sit down beside the projector when you're writing. It's easier to write this way and you won't block anyone's view.

- Use the transparency marking pens to highlight key words, parts of a diagram, etc., either before class or as you describe them.

- Turn off the projector when you're no longer referring to the transparency. The image on the screen distracts from what you are saying.

Special Hints for Using 35-MM SLIDE PROJECTORS:

- Check out the projector before class to see that it works and to make sure it is properly focused. Some models have zoom lenses. In that case make sure the projected image fills the screen without going past the sides of the screen.

- Raise the front of the projector to position the image at the top of the screen. If the projector is going to be used from the rear of the room, and people are going to be sitting in front of it, have it high enough to project over their heads.

- Make a trial run before class to make sure all slides are there and in proper sequence and to make sure the mechanism is operating smoothly. Slides sometimes get hung up and jam the tray.

- Make a couple of practice runs to get familiar with the slides and to practice any explanation you have to give. This will give you a good feel for the time to allow for each slide.

- If your projector doesn't automatically leave the screen dark when no slide is in the slide tray slot, insert blackout slides. These are usually used at the start and end of the slide sequence. This avoids the bright flash of light on the screen.

- Adjust the light level in the room so the projected image is easily seen and there is still a low level of light for note-taking.

- Give the participants enough time to view the slide before moving on to the next one — 10 to 15 seconds is a good rule of thumb. If you're explaining or discussing what's on the slide, this is no problem.

- Use a remote control to advance the slides. Get a cord long enough to allow you to control the projector from the front of the room. A focusing button on the remote control is desirable.

Audio-Visual Aids

Audio-visual aids add the dimension of recorded sound to the visuals. This relieves the course leader of having to do the narration, and allows the use of professional actors or people who are recognized experts in their fields. Audio-visuals can tell a story, pose a problem, explain a process which, in turn, can stimulate discussion and analysis. The most commonly used forms of audio-visual aids are the 16-mm film, videotape, and 35-mm slides with audio tape. Again, let's look at some common mistakes in their use.

Common Mistakes When Using AUDIO-VISUALS:

Letting the audio-visual do the teaching: There is a certain temptation when we don't have too much expertise in the topic to let the audio-visual do all the teaching. It gets introduced, shown, then the course leader moves on to the next topic with the mistaken belief that the participants have learned.

To overcome this, look at your lesson plan and see how

the a/v fits in, plan your introduction for it and develop some discussion questions to follow it. Make it part of the lesson — not an appendage to it.

It's movie time! Use of films and videotapes can create the impression of "going to the movies." That is, participants look at them as sources of entertainment rather than learning and pay attention accordingly.

To overcome this, give them something to do during the viewing. Give them questions to be answered, points to look for, characters to concentrate on, and so forth. This not only helps you bring out the learning points, it heightens interest.

Something breaks down: Audio-visual aids being a combination of electrical, electronic and mechanical elements, are prone to breakdowns. A lamp burns out, a slide jams, the video picture has lines in it, etc.

To overcome this, check it out ahead of time — the projector, the film or videotape, the slides. Have some spare parts and have a technician on call in case your measures don't work. Also, have alternative activities in mind. When going over your lesson plan ask yourself, "What will I do if this (a/v) doesn't work? You may be able to plan a group discussion or other activity.

The participants fail to see the value of it: Some a/v presentations show situations that are out of context with the participants' environment — office supervisors may not identify with a situation concerning a shop foreman; manufacturing people can't relate to something showing a salesman in action. As a result, they mentally turn off.

To overcome this, introduce it in a way that ties the *process* being demonstrated into the participants' environment. Tell them it's about a shop foreman or a pharmaceutical salesman but to look for areas where what that person is doing can be applied to their jobs.

Boredom sets in: Some films and videotapes can be quite lengthy which can lead to people losing interest, getting restless and even falling asleep.

To overcome this, shorten the segments. Look for places

in the film or videotape or slide/tape where you can stop it and hold a brief discussion about an important point that has been illustrated. Then continue to the next logical stopping point and repeat the process. In this way, it becomes a true learning tool.

Special Hints for Using
FILMS & VIDEOTAPES:

These are being considered together because there are so many hints which are common to both.

- Check out the equipment beforehand to make sure it's working properly. With the movie projector, make sure you have a take-up reel of proper capacity and replacement projection and exciter lamps. With the videotape, make sure the monitor and tape player are properly connected and the monitor is set to the appropriate channel (usually 3 or 4).

- Position the movie screen or video monitor so that all participants can easily see it. If the movie projector has a zoom lens, adjust it to fill the screen without going past the sides. If a videotape setup, set the monitor high enough for comfortable viewing.

- Preview the film or videotape. This does two things: familiarizes you with its content and checks its condition. Never show a film or videotape without having seen it yourself. A damaged film should be repaired or replaced; a defective videotape should be replaced.

- Have the film or videotape loaded and ready to go before class starts. Advance the film or videotape to the start of the action.

- Adjust the sound level and, on videotape equipment, the color and tint controls.

- If you plan to stop the film or videotape at various points for discussion, make a notation of the dialogue or scene just prior to that point so you can listen or look for it as a cue. With a videotape player, go through the tape ahead of time, identify those points where you want to stop and write down the number which appears on the counter. (Make sure it's at 0000 when you start the tape.) Use that number as your cue.

- Make the film or videotape a learning experience. Plan your introduction, tell the participants what to look for, give them written questions to answer as they view it, assign small groups to pay particular attention to specific characters or to look for specific aspects. Plan questions to stimulate discussion at the points where you want to stop and to use at the end.

- Stay around during the showing even if you've seen it umpteen times. Something might go wrong with the equipment. If you're not there no one will know what to do. Also, your presence indicates your interest and underscores the value of the piece.

- If the items are going to be used as part of out-of-class activities where the groups will work on their own, make sure at least one member of the group is fully checked out on the operation of the equipment and knows whom to go to for help if something goes wrong.

Special Hints for Using 35-MM SLIDE/TAPE:

Most of the equipment hints already covered apply to the slide projector and audiotape player, but there are some things peculiar to this method.

- Check the slide tray for damage and do a test run with the projector to make sure the slide-change mechanism works smoothly.

- If you're using an audiotape with an audible tone to signal when to change slides, practice using it several times to get into the proper rhythm. That way the slides will keep up with the narration. Also, use a remote-control cable so you don't have to stand next to the projector.

- If you're using an audiotape with a built-in inaudible tone to automatically advance the slides, make sure the proper connection is made between the tape player and slide projector. Also, make sure the inaudible tone works on your tape player. The most commonly used signals are 50 Hz and 1000 Hz. If your equipment is designed for 1000 Hz and the tape has a 50 Hz signal (or vice versa), the slides *will not* advance.

SEASONINGS

Seasonings

Of all the ingredients in a recipe, the most important are the seasonings. Perfect seasoning gives sparkle and zest to dishes and many chefs owe their fame to their use. Seasonings should be used with discretion. They should enhance the flavor of the dish, not overwhelm it and, because individual tastes vary so much, no recipe can really do more than suggest the right amount.

The same holds true for the learning experience. The basic ingredients provide the learning, but the seasonings provide that extra step that makes people come back for more. The selection of seasonings available to the course leader is not as great or as varied as for the chef, but there are several which have a major impact on the session.

Personal Style and Approach

This is the most important seasoning for any learning experience. This is the one seasoning that is impossible not to use since every course leader has a personal style and approach. It's just that some are more effective than others. Some of the key elements to this seasoning are:

CARING — The effective course leader cares about the participants as well as the course. This person *knows* that he or she can't *make* people learn but can only *help* people learn. So, this course leader fights the temptation to "teach" what he or she knows the participants should learn and, instead, creates a psychological climate which enables them to learn for themselves. This course leader also cares enough about the participants to protect their self-esteem. The climate is one which encourages experimentation without fear of failure — no one looks bad in class — no one is going to be put in a position of embarrassment. The climate is supportive. If a participant tries out the new knowledge or skill and blows it, the course leader helps the participant find out what went wrong and what could be done differently next time — then provides a next time! By the same token, the standards which the participants have to meet are high. This includes their level of participation, the effort they put into their own learning, the degree to which they help fellow participants, promptness in attendance and completion of home-work assignments, and a host of other things which are indicative of their willingness to be part of the learning experience.

ENTHUSIASM — Enthusiasm, or the lack of it, is contagious. If you come in and start class projecting the image, "Well, this is something we're supposed to do, so let's get on with it and get it over," you'll get so little participation that you'll probably be able to end your session in half the time. If, on the other hand, you project the image, "Hey, I've got something exciting for you ... that's really going to help you. And, we're going to learn how to do it in a way that's interesting, involving and fun," you're going to have a class full of participants eager to learn. How do you do this? Not so much through your words as through your face, voice and body. A face that's animated, smiling, with changing expressions; a voice that's clear, firm, that accents some words and syllables and downplays others, that varies in speed to achieve emphasis, picking up at times, slowing down at times; a body that's mobile, moving around when necessary, using gestures, using hands and arms to give emphasis. All these elements are used to communicate a vibrance to the people in the audience, one which they will return.

HUMOR — Learning can and should be enjoyable ... be fun. Humor is a vital force in the classroom. Not in the sense of telling jokes, stories or anecdotes, although there are times when one helps make a learning point. Effective humor occurs naturally in the course of the session ... a comment someone makes, a situation which occurs unexpectedly. Classes in which there is no humor are deadly. Be cautious though. Humor is usually at someone's expense; it can end up being embarrassing. If you want to inject some humor, make yourself the butt of the joke. If you carry a fist full of marking pens and accidentally drop the cap of one, bend over to pick it up and make some funny comment about your clumsiness. Humor can become destructive, particularly in the form of zingers. If participants start zinging each other in class, step in and call a halt to it... "Look. We can have fun in class and enjoy ourselves and learn a heck of a lot. But, let's not do it at someone else's expense. The ground rule is: If you've got to zing someone, zing me. Just remember ... I don't get mad, but I do get even."

LISTENING — Active listening encourages an open and frank climate for communication and the effective course leader is an active listener. The listening is not judgmental. When a participant makes a contribution and it is way off base, the course leader doesn't say, "That's a dumb remark!" or, "You don't know what you're talking about." Instead, he or she will say something like, "I don't quite follow that. Can you explain it a little more?" and then probes a little to get at the participant's line of reasoning. The effective course leader also tests his or her understanding by paraphrasing what was said, particularly if the participant has difficulty in phrasing the question or comment clearly.

Subject Matter Experts (SME)

The SME is another key ingredient. It can add a taste which varies from subtle to overwhelming. And, like strong spices and herbs, the amount you use depends on how strongly you want it to influence your end product. Use too little and it has no impact — use too much and it overpowers the other ingredients.

The subject matter experts we are considering are usually operating managers with expertise in a specific function or specialists with expertise in the application of a process, product or technique. An example of the former would be the Manager of Quality Control and an example of the latter, a specialist in designing spread-sheet applications using the personal computer. The SME may be used for out-of-class assignments, or be asked to participate during the class session.

Using SMEs for Out-of-Class Assignments

With this application we don't have to worry too much about the seasoning being overwhelming. It's like marinating meat prior to using it to prepare your dish — it tenderizes the meat while adding flavors. However, these flavors are controlled through the addition of other ingredients during the preparation of the dish. The chef also controls the flavor by selecting the ingredients of the marinade and the length of time the meat marinates. And, just as a recipe suggests these ingredients and time, your lesson plan will usually suggest the type of experts needed and the amount of time that should be scheduled.

One major use of the SME out of class is through interviewing. The participants meet with the SME either individually, in pairs or as small groups. They use a list of suggested questions or a list of specific issues important to an understanding of the topic. Using these they are able to draw on the SME's knowledge and experience. This information is then processed by the participants and provides a basis for discussion in class. For this process to work effectively, the SME needs to be prepared. He or she should know who will be coming, for how long and what kind of information the participants will be looking for. One way to do this would be to give the SME a copy of the assignment instructions being used by the class.

Another use of the SME out of class is for technical guidance in the operation of equipment, the use of a process or technique or a complicated software package. Again, this needs to be arranged in advance to ensure that the SME is available at the required time and knows what assistance to provide.

Using SMEs during the Class Session

This use of the seasoning requires constant monitoring. Like any seasoning used in the actual cooking process, it's better to start with a small amount, taste it, then add more until you get the desired flavor. You can always add more, but once it's in there, it's impossible to remove! More dishes have been ruined during the cooking stage from a heavy hand with the seasonings.

The reason you bring an SME into class is to enrich the content with firsthand experience and practical insight. The SME isn't there to make a formal presentation. Unfortunately, some course leaders let the SME take over and, because he or she doesn't have the facilitating skills of the course leader, the session becomes a hard-sell lecture. After all, the SME is proud of his or her function and is always looking for converts. The course leader needs to set the ground rules in advance. Usually we want the SME to listen to what the participants are saying and to react by clarifying misunderstandings, resolving contradictions, providing specific information or examples and adding important information which may have been overlooked.

Using SMEs in Round-Table Discussions

A variation of the in-class SME. This involves the participation of several SMEs and is valuable when you want to give the participants exposure to a variety of functions, specialties or viewpoints. It is usually done in a question-and-answer format and the questions may be from individual participants or ones prepared by the class as a whole. Some good guidelines for this are:

- Questions which can be answered in 3 minutes or less
- Questions which will bring out ideas and opinions as well as facts
- An equal number of questions for each SME.

The visiting SMEs also need information as to what kinds of questions the participants may ask and the topic or topics being covered. The course leader's job during the discussion is that of discussion moderator. That is, making the introductory comments, getting the discussion started, and making sure it ends on time.

Using SMEs for Guest Presentations

This is an important variation of the subject matter expert. It's similar to the head chef using a salad chef to prepare a Caesar Salad or a flambé chef to prepare Steak Diane — each has a specialty to add to the preparation of the meal.

In the class, the SME does make a formal presentation, usually in the form of a lecture. It may or may not be accompanied by visuals. The presentation should be relatively short — 20 to 30 minutes — and be followed by a discussion or question-and-answer period of 15 to 20 minutes. To derive optimum value from the SME, make sure he or she knows what information is to be presented, how much time is being allowed for the presentation and the type of class interaction which will follow the presentation. The participants also should be informed of the content in advance to enable them to think about questions they might want to bring up. Again, the course leader's task is one of control and you may have to come up with some diplomatic ways of letting the SME know when he or she is running over the allotted time. This is where judgment comes into play. If it's beneficial, you may let the SME continue; if he or she is getting off track or is just droning on and on, you will have to step in and call time.

All in all, the subject matter expert can add a unique flavor to the class session.

CONTROLS

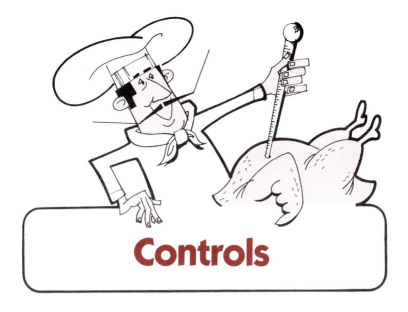

Controls

When preparing and cooking the dish, the chef doesn't assume that everything will go as planned — controls are used throughout the process. Some of the controls are obvious — a thermometer to check ingredient or oven temperature, a timer to indicate when a particular phase should be completed. Most controls, however, are much more subtle — knowing what the dish should look like at each stage of preparation, using smell to detect when something is in danger of being overcooked, tasting to make sure the seasonings are right and so forth.

The course leader, too, has to use controls to make sure everything goes smoothly. Some are used before the class starts, some at the start of class, some during class and others at the end of class. Let's look at some of the details.

Before Class Starts

Think what it would be like if you went to a top-rated restaurant and ordered Steak Diane for your entree. You have an appetizer, perhaps a salad, maybe a cocktail and some interesting conversation with your companion. You glance up, see the flambé chef approaching with his cart and rub your hands in eager anticipation. The cart rolls up, the chef lights the burner and prepares the pan — then looks down at the cart, mumbles something under his breath and dashes away to the kitchen and comes back with a forgotten ingredient. He then mixes the ingredients, gets the pan hot, sears the steak, adds the ingredients then, hitting himself on the forehead, dashes back to the kitchen and returns with the brandy. He gets it ready, adds it to the pan, gets ready to light it — and the burner goes out. Another mad dash, this time for a can of sterno. Are you still at the table or have you said the hell with it and gone outside to the hotdog vendor on the corner? Does this sound far-fetched, exaggerated? If it does, think of all the times you've seen similar occurrences in the classroom. Preparation before the class starts is one of your major controls. Not only your personal preparation in terms of course content and flow, but all the nitty-gritty details of making sure everything is ready and working. Don't take anything for granted — check out these things well before class starts.

ROOM SETUP — Make sure the room is properly set up, that the tables and chairs are in the desired configuration, that the projection screen and flipchart easels can be easily seen by all participants, that the lighting is adequate and controllable, that the temperature is comfortable but not too warm and, most important but most often neglected, there's a clock on the wall.

EQUIPMENT AND SUPPLIES — Check out your equipment and supplies. Make sure you have all necessary participant materials and enough of them. Have all necessary miscellaneous supplies such as a stapler, three-hole punch, pencil sharpener, pushpins, masking tape, etc. Check out your visual and audio-visual aids (review the hints for using these in the chapter on **Tools**). If you are using PC and/or interactive video workstations, make sure they are set up properly and that you have the correct diskettes and videodisks.

At the Start of Class

What you do at the start of class sets the tone for the rest of the session and even for the rest of the course. You are the authority figure, hence the role model for desired behavior for the course. Therefore, it is important that you:

SET THE STAGE — Greet the participants as they come in, smile, introduce yourself if they don't already know you, chat with them for a few minutes.

START ON TIME — Not all participants will be early or on time, particularly when the course is first starting. The course leader's reaction, "Well, I'll give them a couple of more minutes — I'd like everyone to be here before I start," is a very normal one. However, the pattern this reaction could establish is one that says, "It's okay to be late, class doesn't start on time anyway." If you start on time, regardless of how many participants are there, the tardy ones will be more likely to get the message that they better get there on time if they don't want to lose out on some important information.

CLARIFY EXPECTATIONS — Participants come into the first session carrying a lot of baggage in the form of inappropriate or incorrect expectations about what will happen to them. Get rid of this baggage early! One way would be to take a few minutes to have them form groups of three or four to share expectations and objectives, agree on a few that seem to be in common and prioritize them as to their importance. Ask them to list these on a flipchart page and to have one of the group report to the class. This does several things for you: 1) it gets participants actively involved early, 2) it gives them the chance to think more thoroughly about their expectations and objectives, 3) it starts the group-building process and 4) it lets you know where they are coming from.

You then have the opportunity to talk about which expectations will be met by the course and which will not and to lead into what participants can expect from the course and what will be expected of them. This should include their degree of involvment as individuals, working together effectively as teams, learning from one another's experience, knowledge, viewpoints and opinions, meeting the requirements of the course including any out-of-class activities and the expectation that everyone will contribute to the success of the course.

During the Class

For the most part, your participants' initial attitudes toward you and your course will range from neutral to acceptance with a sprinkling on the skeptical end and a few on the eager end. Outright hostility, fortunately, is rare. The successful course leader is sensitive to the obvious and not-so-obvious signs that indicate potential problems. Isolated occurrences are normal; repeated occurrences signify danger. How you interact with the participants and how you conduct the class can drastically affect this intitial attitude. The successful course leader moves people toward the eager end of the spectrum.

RESPECT — Gaining and maintaining the respect of the participants is critical to the success of the session. Think back to a time in your own experience where something happened to cause you to feel increased respect for the course leader. How did you feel? What effect did it have on your learning? What did you do overtly or covertly to let the course leader know how you felt? How much did you find yourself supporting what he/she said? How involved did you become in class activities? What did you do to contribute to the success of the session? Did you start coming in early and staying late, because you wanted to? These are just a few of the manifestations that indicate heightened respect for the course leader.

Now think back to that time again. What did the course leader do to gain your respect? Did he or she recognize the knowledge and experience that existed within the group and build upon it? Protect the self-esteem of someone who tried something new and failed? Let you fail but helped you learn from it? Treated the group with respect? Helped you find ways to apply what you were learning? Was knowledgeable but didn't come on as "the expert" who had the only right answers? Made you feel you were part of an exciting experience? Again, these are just a few of the things that can create respect from the particpants. An interesting experiment would be to ask several of your associates what would make them respect a course leader, and make a list of their responses. Then put that list over your desk and make a solemn vow, "These are the things I am going to do in my class."

INTEREST — The successful course leader also knows that interest in what the participants are doing can help them get through a long stretch of time. Again, think back to your own experience as a participant when you and your fellow participants were involved in the class activities. How conscious were you of the passage of time? How much did you see of activities such as people slouched in their chairs tapping fingers or pencils on the table, people engaged in side conversations unrelated to the topic at hand, people withdrawn or daydreaming, people watching the clock? The odds are you saw little or none of that behavior.

The successful course leader is sensitive to these nonverbal signs and knows that while you can expect some people to do these things occasionally, if a lot of people do them often, there is a problem. Again, what did your course leader do? Did he show enthusiasm through his voice and body language? Did she ask questions and get people involved in discussions? Were visuals and audio-visuals used? Were small group activities used to get people up on their feet and out of the main class room? These are the kinds of things available to course leaders to keep things interesting and moving. In a sense, they act as controls because they prevent boredom and the resultant adverse effects on the course. Most of these activities are, or should be, built into your lesson plan. Use them to create a sense of movement, purpose and learning.

CHECKING ON RESULTS — The experienced chef, when baking a cake, takes control steps such as setting the oven temperature and the timer. He/she also knows that a final check must be made to make sure that the cake is done. He/she inserts a thin wire into the center of the cake. If it comes out clean, the cake is done; if batter sticks to it, it needs more time.

The successful course leader also needs to check results. This is done by asking questions to test the participants' understanding and by asking for examples to test for application. (The chapter on **Questioning** goes into more detail on how to do this.)

"PROBLEM" PARTICIPANTS — The actions of particular participants may require the use of controls. These are much more sensitive because if the control is poorly applied, the aftereffects can poison the entire class. The successful course leader is alert to the behavior and tries to correct the situation early. Some of the more common types are:

✓ **The Limelight Grabber** — This is the individual who dominates the class, who always has a hand up to answer your questions and who overwhelms anyone else trying to make a contribution to the discussion. Most of the time the intent is not malicious — he or she is so caught up in the process that the words come bubbling out. This is a difficult situation because, on one hand, you don't want to turn off this enthusiasm but, on the other hand, you don't want it to dominate the group.

When this behavior becomes a problem, some of your options are: not see the raised hand or hear the voice; recognize the desire to make a contribution but say something like, "I'd like to get some other viewpoints first," or, "Let's get some input from some of the others"; avoid eye contact with the individual when asking the group for input; direct your questions to specific individuals. If these messages don't get through, you may have to talk with the individual after class and explain that while this enthusiasm is greatly appreciated, it is getting in the way of others who are also trying to make contributions. Appeal to the individual to give others a chance.

In the relatively rare case when the Limelight Grabber is maliciously motivated, the same actions can apply. However, the out-of-class talk may need to come sooner. In this talk, try to find out why the individual is behaving this way — there may be something you can do to correct the cause of the problem. If whatever you say or do does not change the individual's behavior, you may have to fall back on the final solution — "Don't bother coming back to class."

✓ **The Assistant Course Leader** — Similar in nature to the friendly Limelight Grabber but differently motivated. Not only does this person want to make a contribution, he/she wants to help you teach! While this propensity can be useful if, indeed, the individual has the knowledge or skills you are trying to get across, it can get in the way if he/she constantly interrupts to amplify on what you are saying. And there are times when your fingers itch for a throat when, after carefully leading the class down a line of reasoning toward an "A-Ha," the Assistant Course Leader blurts out the answer.

Again, a difficult situation. This person is not trying to disrupt the class. On the contrary, he/she is trying to be helpful. This desire and knowledge can be productively channeled. If you have participants who are having difficulty catching on to an idea or application, use this person to help them. Put them on the same team in a small group activity. When appropriate, ask the Assistant Course Leader to explain a concept in terms more meaningful to the group. Sometimes you can talk to this person after class and, in conspiratorial tones, explain that you sometimes deliberately set the class up to make a learning point and that he/she can help by not giving it away.

The Inveterate Skeptic — This is the individual who takes nothing at face value. It's not that he/she is trying to be deliberately disruptive, it's just that everything has to be proved. This person can cause you to fall into the trap of being "the expert" if you feel you have to have all the answers. Use the class to field the Skeptic's objections, particularly the Assistant Course Leader if you have one. If an application is questioned, ask if someone can cite an example of successful application in the immediate organization. Have some examples yourself — gathering them should be part of your homework. Ask the individual to elaborate on his/her concern, you may find that there is an element of misunderstanding that can be corrected. In any event, *don't argue — you're bound to lose!* And that can weaken the respect the others hold for you.

The Rambler — This individual is a distant relative of the Limelight Grabber and the Assistant Course Leader; he/she shows the same compulsion to talk. When called on to give an example to illustrate a point, the Rambler goes into excruciating detail, starting (so it seems) with the year he/she was born. When asked to comment on a statement made by another participant, expresses his/her opinion surrounded by many qualifications, conditions and stipulations. It takes this person five minutes to give a 30-second answer.

Another sensitive issue, one you hope won't happen too often. When it does happen though, you can tactfully interrupt with a question or a statement summarizing what has been said or wait for a pause, then rephrase the last statement made, and direct a question to another participant.

The Timid Soul — This is the individual who attends the class but who doesn't participate in it. Usually tries to blend into the crowd, generally looks uncomfortable and even a bit fearful, and looks relieved when someone else answers your questions.

Sensitivity and empathy are called for here. One way to draw this person out is to ask for an opinion rather than an answer. If someone makes a statement that lends itself to discussion, turn to the Timid Soul and say, "(name), how do you feel about that?" Another way is to ask him/her a question which contains the right answer. Reinforce any answer or comment this person makes with comments such as "Good idea," "Thanks for that insight," or even probe a little with, "That's an interesting observation, build on it a little more." The more this person hears his/her voice, the more likely participation will increase.

At the End of Class

The chef has one final test for results; the customer's response to the meal. If the chef has succeeded, it's, "My compliments to the chef!" If not, it's complaints like, "The food was cold, underdone, overdone, tasted lousy, was greasy, etc." The chef who cares will seek out this information. The course leader who cares will look for it, too.

The successful course leader is interested in how well the content came across particularly in terms of what the participants have identified as application to their own situations. Thus, the course leader will get examples of application from the participants. If you've tested for understanding and application throughout the session, this will be just a review. Then, have them take a couple of minutes to put these applications into writing as part of an "action plan" which can be implemented later at an appropriate time.

A Final Note

Just as the chef who has labored long to create a culinary masterpiece looks for feedback from those who have eaten it, the successful course leader wants to know "How Am I Doing?"

One way you might do this is to use the **"How Am I Doing?"** form in the back of this book. Use it as is, modify the questions, add to them, eliminate some of them, but get yourself some feedback ... it's invaluable!

RECIPES

Recipes

Using a Recipe

The effective chef follows a set routine before beginning to mix ingredients for a dish. This includes:

- Reading the recipe carefully and, if any part of the process is unfamiliar, reviewing information or instructions on it
- Making sure the necessary ingredients and equipment are on hand
- Having ingredients at proper temperature
- Having ingredients set out and measured, if required
- Making sure the oven is preheated if it is to be used
- Preparing pots and pans, as required
- Having the cookbook handy and open to the recipe and consulting it as the work progresses.

What does the effective course leader do? Exactly the same thing! There is a set routine to be followed before convening the class. You need to:

- Read the course leader guide carefully and, if any part of the *process* is unfamiliar, seek clarification either in the leader guide or use the material in this book.
- Make sure the necessary ingredients and equipment are on hand — copies of handouts, transparencies, video-

tapes, texts, projectors, PC workstations, questions, flipcharts, etc.

- Make sure everything is ready for use — that the equipment is properly set up and operating; that spare parts such as projector lamps are available; that preprepared transparencies, slides, flipcharts are ready for use
- See that there is enough of everything, particularly handouts, exercise instructions, team assignments, etc.
- Check the classroom environment — not too hot, not too cold, not too noisy, comfortable but not so comfortable that people are too relaxed
- Make sure that any special requirements are available, particularly guest speakers or participating subject matter experts and that they understand what is expected of them
- Keep your leader guide handy and open to the proper place. Don't be afraid to refer to it, no one expects you to have it memorized. Have any notes you've made to yourself clear and easy to read, and finally
- Have faith in the process ... **It works!!**

> Following are some basic recipes for creating successful learning experiences. Use them as a guide — modify them to fit your lesson plan and your personal style. Remember, the chef uses basic recipes and through experience, knowledge and experimentation, creates culinary masterpieces. You can do the same.

INTRODUCING TOPICS

Use for introducing a topic, new point, concept, etc.

Ingredients

- Lesson Plan
- Lecturette Method
- Your Knowledge
- Group's Knowledge/Experience
- Examples
- Questions
- Visual Aids

Procedure

Try to stimulate immediate interest. You can do this by posing a hypothetical or actual situation or problem, or by referring to a previously covered topic and bridging into the new topic by showing how they are related. Examples used to illustrate your points should be from the workplace; questions should be the content-specific, test-for-understanding type. Visual aids such as flipchart, chalk- or whiteboard, overhead projector, etc. are optional.

I. Introducing New Information — Verbally bridge from a previous topic into the new one explaining *What* and *Why*. For example:

> "We've looked at (topic) in pretty good detail, now let's look at some applications to our business and see how they affect what we do."

II. Bridging from a Previous Session or Assignment — Verbally bridge from a previous topic or assignment as before and amplify points being made. Questions reviewing the previous topic or assignment are a good way to do this. The use of visual aids such as flipcharts, overhead transparencies or 35-mm slides can be a helpful way to illustrate your points. Well-chosen examples are also useful. For instance, if you are building on a preclass assignment on types of questions:

"Asking questions is one of the most effective means of getting information, analyzing it and getting cooperation

INTRODUCING TOPICS (cont.)

from others. One of our goals is to help you learn useful types of questions and experience their effects. Your pre-class reading dealt with two major types of questions — 'Open' and 'Closed.' "

Q. "How do they differ?" (Get responses.)

Q. "What would determine when you would ask an open or closed question?" (Get responses.)

"Let's take a look at a situation where a line of questioning results in getting cooperation from a reluctant individual." (Show videotape.)

III. Building on Existing Knowledge and Experience — Here you can use questions or pose a situation and ask the class to respond. You should have a series of questions prepared to get the class to bring out the points you want. As an example, if the course is on Supervision and you want to introduce the topic, "Job Instruction Training," you might use this sequence:

Q. "How effective is a new employee the first few days on the job?"
A. "Not very."
Q. "Why not?"
A. "Doesn't really know what to do."
Q. "Okay, so then what has to be done?"
A. "Has to be trained."
Q. "You're the supervisor. What's your role in this?"
A. "To train him or see that he gets trained."
Q. "How do you do that?"
A. (Varied)
Q. "If you had a simple, fast way of getting that employee up to speed on the job, what would be the benefits to you?"
A. (Varied, but positive.)

"Okay, let's look at such a method. We'll see what it is, how it works, and get some practice in using it."

LECTURE

The traditional lecture approach does not stimulate participation, hence should either be kept short (**Lecturette**) or designed to promote participation (**Participative Lecture**). Here are recipes for each approach.

I. Lecturette — Use for introducing new topics, expanding on ideas and supplying new information.

Ingredients

- Lesson Plan
- Your Knowledge
- Examples
- Visual Aids

Procedure

This is a short (less than 10 minutes) version of the lecture. It enables you to get into a topic quickly, expand on points being made during the session and summarize at the end of the session. Examples are useful to illustrate points as are visual aids such as flipchart, chalk- or whiteboard, overhead transparencies or 35-mm slides. This is essentially one-way communication; you're not looking for participation from the class. For example, if you are describing the course to your participants in the first class session, you might say something like this:

- "Each session consists of these activities:"
  (Show visual with activity titles; briefly describe each.)
- "The objectives of the course are to:"
  (Show visual listing objectives; briefly explain each.)
- "The methods we'll use during the course are:"
  (Show visual and briefly describe methods.)

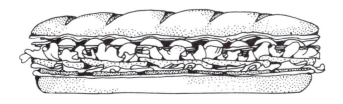

LECTURE (cont.)

II. Participative Lecture — For use when you have information or knowledge the participants haven't but you want to get their involvement.

Ingredients

- Lesson Plan
- Your Knowledge
- Group's Knowledge/ Experience
- Questions & Questioning Sequence
- Examples
- Visual Aids, as appropriate
- Demonstration, as appropriate

Procedure

The participative lecture is a combination of you and the participants talking. While you are presenting new information, use your questions to link this information to what the participants already know. Get them to give you examples and applications. If possible, use visuals to illustrate the points you are making. If some points aren't being brought out by the group you can add them by asking, "What about ____?" If the subject is *Communication* and the topic is Nonverbal Communication and how it affects understanding, you might follow this sequence (use the flipchart, chalk- or whiteboard to record their answers):

Q. "We're all in agreement that talking with someone is a form of communication and that the words spoken transmit meaning (assuming common definitions). But, there are other more subtle, nonverbal communications going on at the same time. What might some of these be?"

A. "Body language; tone of voice; facial expressions."

LECTURE (cont.)

(The following questions should bring a variety of answers.)

Q. "What are some examples of?" (Do for each type.)

Q. "Think back to an experience you've had. How did _____ affect understanding? What happened as a result?"

Q. "What do _____ do to the communication process?"

Q. "How can _____ be used to help the communication process?"

Q. "What conclusions can we draw about the effects of nonverbal communication on achieving desired results?"

Variation — Use demonstration to get a point across. Either demonstrate it yourself or ask someone in the class to do it. It can provide a vivid example of effects. For instance, you can demonstrate how tone of voice or a facial expression can completely change the meaning of the verbal message.

DISCUSSIONS: COURSE-LEADER LED

Use to get involvement, help participants share their knowledge and experience in relation to the topic, build on their knowledge and experience and get them to convince themselves.

Ingredients

- Lesson Plan
- Discussion Method
- Situation or Problem
- Your Knowledge
- Group's Knowledge and Experience
- Examples
- Questions and Questioning Sequence
- Visual Aids, as appropriate
- Listening Skills

General Procedure

The learning experience is much more effective when the activities are learner-centered. That is, the participants are an integral part of the teaching, as well as learning efforts. Group discussions are an excellent way to accomplish this. These discussions may be directed by the course leader or occur within subgroups. Here are three recipes for course-leader-led discussions.

DISCUSSIONS: COURSE-LEADER LED
(cont.)

I. Information-Gathering Discussion — The information flow is primarily between you and the participants. The purpose is to draw on the participants' knowledge and experience and use that to illustrate points, concepts, processes, etc. This is usually done by posing a situation and then asking for ideas, suggestions, solutions. To illustrate: You want to introduce the concept that well-run or well-disciplined organizations have characteristics in common and that these characteristics can be fostered in any group, especially the participants' groups. (Your participants are supervisors.)

> "Many organizations are held up as role models of effective organizations. People enjoy being part of them. There's a lot of competition in gaining membership and membership requirements are quite strict. Yet, many people still want to join. Some examples might be: a 'Big 10' college marching band; the Navy's 'Blue Angels'; a championship ball club; and so on. There's something about these organizations that makes them stand out."

Q. "What are some characteristics that these organizations have in common?"

A. (Write them on the flipchart, chalk- or whiteboard as they are brought out. Get amplification if what the participant is saying is not too clear.)
  — A feeling of belonging   — A lot of time practicing
  — Respect for each other   — Self-discipline
  — Respect for the leader   — Follow the rules
  — Know their jobs   — High standards, etc.

Q. "These are the kinds of things that make these groups outstanding. What would your jobs be like if your units had these characteristics?"

A. "Easier; wouldn't need me; a snap; etc."

DISCUSSIONS: COURSE-LEADER LED
(cont.)

II. Experience-Sharing Discussion — The information flow is primarily among the participants with an occasional input from the course leader. Again, we're drawing on their experience in relation to the topic. As with the Information-Gathering discussion, the group needs to be primed with a situation or a question. The questions usually start out as content-specific then shift to the generic. For instance:

> "You've just seen an unfortunate situation in the video vignette where what could have been a good working relationship between Mike and John degenerated into an argument and a lot of bad feelings."

Q. "Who among you has had a situation like this?"

A. (Look for raised hands; pick out two or three to describe their situations.)

Q. "What caused the problem you had?" (To the individuals.)

A. (Get their answers.)

Q. "What could (name) have done differently to avoid the problem?" (To the group.)

A. (Get them talking among themselves.)

During the course of the discussion you may need to use some booster questions to keep things going, for example:

Q. "What techniques have you found effective?"

Q. "How did you resolve the issue?"

Q. "What's the message in all of this?"

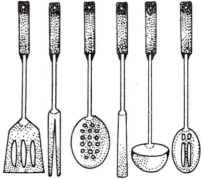

**DISCUSSIONS:
COURSE-LEADER LED**
(cont.)

III. Case-Study Discussion — This is a variation on both the Information-Gathering and Experience-Sharing discussions. The information-gathering comes in analyzing the case and applying the techniques or principles being learned, and the experience-sharing comes in making the transition from the case to practical application on the job. The case provides the situation to be discussed. In our example, the topic is nonverbal communication and the situation is a new employee reporting to work on his first day.

Q. "Voice cues affect the meaning and impact of the message. In the case you read, how did they affect the interaction between Jim, the new employee, and Pete, the old hand?"

Q. "What are some examples of voice cues which block comunication?" (A good place to ask someone to demonstrate a voice cue.)

Q. "Body language is also an important element. What were some examples of body language described in the case?"

Q. "What messages did they communicate?"

Q. "What kinds of body language block communication?"

Q. "What kinds help communication?"

Q. "You have an inexperienced employee and you have to give him a job assignment. What voice cues and body language would you use when delivering your message?"

Q. "Why?"

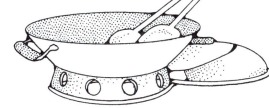

DISCUSSIONS: SMALL-GROUP

Use to build on participants' knowledge and experience, increase individual involvement, provide opportunities for application of what is being learned, generate information to be discussed when the class reassembles.

Ingredients

- Situation or Task Definition
- Team Assignments
- Breakout Room/ Area Assignments
- Equipment & Supplies, as necessary
- Written Instructions
- Group's Knowledge/ Experience
- Time Allocation
- Visual Aids, as appropriate

General Procedure

Small-Group discussions are excellent vehicles for getting everyone involved. In a full-class discussion, some people hang back and don't participate; when they are in small groups, participation is much more likely. There is a sense of commitment to the answers, suggestions, reports they bring back to the class even when there isn't 100% agreement among the group members. A lot of learning goes on in the group as members defend their positions by building on their experience and knowledge.

Types of Small-Group discussions generally used are the Information Gathering/Experience Sharing and the Application. Most of the ingredients listed above are used in either type. The ingredients that differ are: Situation or Task Definition and Written Instructions.

DISCUSSIONS: SMALL-GROUP
(cont.)

I. Information-Gathering/Experience-Sharing — For the Information-Gathering/Experience-Sharing discussion, the situation or task definition may be related to a film or video just seen, a case that was read, some specific topic covered in class, or even used to generate information to build on when introducing a new topic. A simple example would be a session on time-management principles. If you want to make the point that your participants already know a lot about time management, you can do this by giving this small-group assignment (sample of written instructions):

"The team to which you have been assigned has two tasks:

1. Identify and list on the flipchart page the major interferences with the effective use of managerial time.

2. List on the flipchart page the solutions to the identified managerial time problems which are suggested by the team members.

Select a spokesperson to make a presentation to the class.

You have _____ minutes; be back at _____ ."

DISCUSSIONS: SMALL-GROUP
(cont.)

II. Application — For an application exercise, the instructions must be more explicit. For instance, let's say your topic is "The Management Process" and you've been exploring the activities of Planning, Organizing, Staffing, Directing and Controlling as part of the process. You now want to give the participants practice in applying these concepts. The instructions might look something like this:

"You're the manager of an organization which is scheduling a 50% increase in production over the next 12 months. Your task is to identify the following for each of the managerial activities of Planning, Organizing, Staffing, Directing and Controlling:

— Actions a manager must take to carry out the activity
— Information the manager needs for these actions
— Timing of the actions
— Knowledge and skill needed for effective actions.

Work individually for a short time, thinking in terms of the managerial impact of a 50% increase on your operation. Pool your thoughts through group discussion and prepare a flipchart presentation for the entire group.

— Select a member of the group to act as spokesperson, preferably someone who has not had that opportunity yet.
You have _____ minutes; be back at _____ ."

A variation on the application exercise is a case study where the participants are assigned roles, given information specific to that role and are instructed to use the process being learned to analyze the data and prepare recommendations.

EXPERIENTIAL

Use to have the participants experience the concepts being learned, to illustrate a principle, to demonstrate the effects of an action or actions and to help develop skills through practice.

Ingredients (Select, as appropriate to the application.)

- Situation or Task Definition
- Equipment & Supplies, as necessary
- Your Knowledge
- Group's Knowledge/ Experience
- Written Instructions, as necesary
- Process, Method or Technique to be applied
- Team Assignments, as necessary
- Breakout Rooms/Areas, as necessary
- Visual Aids, as necessary
- Debriefing Process

General Procedure

In the classroom, participants generally get an intellectual understanding of what is being covered; they know *what* to do, *why* to do it and can even describe *how* to do it, but it really doesn't sink in until they actually *do* it. Now they *know* what it's like to do it, find out that they really didn't understand it as well as they thought and sharpen their application skills by learning from their mistakes. The experiential situation could be as simple as you assuming the role of a dissatisfied employee and backing one of your participants into the proverbial corner, or as complex as planning, designing and setting up an assembly line to produce a product. Your imagination is the limiting factor. Here are some suggestions for setting up experiential situations.

EXPERIENTIAL
(cont.)

I. Role-Play — An effective experiential vehicle since it can be used to help people experience concepts and techniques, particularly behavioral and emotional, and to give participants the opportunity to practice using a technique. Some participants may feel uncomfortable or even intimidated by the idea of having to role-play so a learning climate that says "It's okay to blow it" is essential. Among the ground rules you have to establish are:

> — No one is going to be made to look bad
> — No one is going to be embarrassed
> — We're here to help each other learn to do it better
> — We're going to get and give feedback on what was done well and what needs improvement.

A major job you have when using the role-play technique is to act as a coach. You need to be thoroughly familiar with the behaviors or skills being practiced and must, with the group, provide helpful feedback on performance — what went well and what could be done differently next time to get better results. The psychological climate is critical — it has to be one that says, "It's okay to make a mistake, we learn more from our mistakes than from our successes." The questioning technique is valuable for debriefing a role play. Ask the role players such questions as:

- "In your role, how did you feel about the results of this discussion?"
- "What should, could have (name) done differently?"
- "What are you going to do as a result of this discussion?"

Ask the group:

- "How well did (name) do in following the process?"
- "What could have been done differently or better to achieve the desired outcome?"

EXPERIENTIAL (cont.)

In this critique or feedback phase, it is vital to protect the self-esteem of the role players particularly if it didn't go so well. All feedback must be supportive and designed to improve performance. Sometimes, members of a class come down hard on the role players. Control this by reminding them that they are there to help, not to criticize. Remember, the learning occurs as a result of the discussion following the experience, not from the experience itself.

II. Behavior-Modeling — This is an adaptation of the role-playing technique. It differs in that key actions are provided as guides to follow and the use of these is modeled in a video presentation. In role-playing, the guidelines provided may be very sketchy and leave a lot to the imagination of the role players; in behavior-modeling, the guidelines are very detailed. They are based on what people who are effective in conducting these discussions do. Thus, they are known dimensions which have been proven through application. The role-play part of behavior-modeling gives the participants the opportunity to practice following the key actions using actual situations from the job and to receive feedback on how they did. The feedback sequence is the same as that described under Role-Play.

The typical sequence of events in a behavior-modeling session is:

- An overview of the topic; why it's important

- Introducing the key actions that are to be followed and why they are important

- Giving the participants some time to study these and to identify specific on-job situations where they can be applied

- Viewing and discussing the video role model

- Practice using the key actions and getting feedback on results.

EXPERIENTIAL
(cont.)

Some organizations have developed their own behavior-modeling courses and others use purchased courses, thus there are a number of variations on this sequence and differences in the course materials supplied to the participants. Each course also has a leader's guide with specific instructions. These are what you will use in leading the course. Again, your job is to act as a coach and help the participants learn from their experiences.

III. Interviewing — This is an excellent way to help participants get the real world perspective on the topic they are studying. It takes what would normally be a book-learning experience and makes it a pragmatic experience. It gives the participants the opportunity to meet and get to know people in positions of leadership and helps them learn from their experience.

The interview can be an individual assignment, a pair's assignment or done by a group of three or four. The size of your class would be the determining factor. If you had a class of 16, you wouldn't want the interviewees to be hit with 16 separate interviews, so you could go with teams of four. If you only had eight or nine participants, you might elect to use pairs or trios.

Clear task instructions are essential for the success of this technique. The participants need to know:

- Whom to talk to
- How to prepare for the interview
- What questions to ask during the interview
- What to do with the information gathered
- How long to spend with the person being interviewed.

EXPERIENTIAL
(cont.)

Whom to talk to depends on the topic. If the course is on front-line supervision, operating foremen/supervisors, or people who have served in that capacity, are likely candidates. If the course is on manufacturing operations, those who manage each operation are good sources of information. If the course is on a technical discipline, a local practitioner is good to talk with. Your own experience and knowledge of your organization should be a good guide for likely interview candidates.

How to prepare for the interview might include instructions to read or review text material, articles or other related background information; to find out a little about the job responsibilities of that postition; to become thoroughly familiar with the questions to be asked, etc.

In general, questions to be asked should be provided. Since this is an important part of the learning experience, it needs to be structured to ensure that the required information is discussed. The questions used would depend on the topic and the learning objectives. For example, if the topic is "Supervision," some questions that might be asked of an operating supervisor are:

- "What are the responsibilities of a supervisor in an operation?"
- "How does a supervisor spend his/her time on a given day?"
- "What key measurements must a supervisor meet?"
- "What aspects of the supervisor's job make it challenging?"

Answers to questions like these can be found in the classroom ... hearing them from the "horse's mouth" makes them much more meaningful.

EXPERIENTIAL
(cont.)

After the information is gathered, the participants need to know what to do with it. In most cases, they prepare summaries which they report to the class in the next session. Sometimes only a written report is required. The nature of the task is determined by what you're trying to accomplish.

How long the interview is also depends on what you're trying to accomplish. Most interviews range from one to two hours, however, remember, these are busy people who have just so much time to spare.

In many cases it is also advisable to give the prospective interviewee information on what the participants are looking for and the questions they'll ask. This gives the interviewee the chance to prepare for the meeting and to help the meeting along if the participant has difficulty with his/her end. It also is a time saver ... answers to the questions can be readily available.

IV. Games and Simulations — These are usually combinations of role-play and case study. They can take different forms: paper-and-pencil exercises, in-basket exercises, board games, construction projects, etc. They all involve the analysis of data, the application of the concepts or process/technique being learned and the making of decisions. At their simplest, the activity runs from one to three hours, the members of the team all play the same role and the decisions are reached through consensus. At their most complex, the activity may extend over the length of the course, each member of the team is assigned a different role and is given information specific to that role. The task is working under an assigned (or team-determined) leader, work together as a team, under realistic conditions, and produce a product.

EXPERIENTIAL
(cont.)

While most of the ingredients for **Games** and **Simulations** can be drawn from the initial list under the **Experiential** heading, some special ingredients may be required, such as:

For Games

- Game Objective (desired end result)
- Playing Rules
- Background Information, on which to base decisions
- Special Instructions, as required
- Playing Time Limits
- Game Pieces, if a board game
- Exercise Booklets, if a paper-and-pencil exercise
- Book Answers, as appropriate

For Simulations

- Description of Tasks, to be accomplished and desired end result
- Rules, under which the tasks are to be accomplished
- Background Information: by role, for the simulated organization, the product or service provided, etc.
- A list of Decisions to be made
- Materials, if a construction or assembly project
- Performance Deadline, if time is a factor

Games and **Simulations** are generally self-run. That is, once you've given the teams their materials and instructions, they take it from there. All you need to do is check on their progress occasionally. For simulations extending over several weeks, intermediate reporting points are usually built in. These reports keep you apprised of progress. For lengthy simulations, each stage of the simulation requires application of what has been learned to date and, particularly, in the current class session.

INDIVIDUAL LEARNING EXPERIENCES

Use to provide practice through application, to bring individuals up to a common level of understanding before formal class sessions start and where small-group activities are not feasible.

Ingredients

- Situation or Task Definition
- Equipment & Supplies, as necessary
- Individual's Knowledge/ Experience
- Written Instructions, as necessary
- Process, Method or Technique to be applied
- Courseware or Software, as necessary

General Procedure

Individual learning experiences expand the overall learning process. While some of these may be included as in-class activities, they are usually assigned as out-of-class work. This allows valuable class time to be reserved for group learning experiences. When we hear "out-of-class assignments," we generally think of the traditional "homework": reading a text, chapter, article and preparing a report or answering some questions or doing some research and writing a paper. The assignments we're talking about here, though, require a more proactive or interactive response. Among these are interviewing, interactive video (tape or disk), the personal computer and associated software, and the use of personal logbooks or diaries.

I. Interviewing — The ingredients and technique are the same as those listed under the **Experiential** application of interviewing. There may be a little more pressure on the participant since the safety in numbers aspect has been removed, but basically the process is the same.

INDIVIDUAL LEARNING EXPERIENCES (cont.)

II. Interactive Video — This is a relatively new, high-tech approach to individual learning. At its simplest, it provides new information, tests for recall or understanding, compares the individual's answer to the book answer and provides feedback on accuracy. In its more complex forms, it can simulate actual conditions, require the individual to make a decision, then branch to a sequence that shows the results of that decision.

There is usually provision for keeping a record of the participant's progress, including accuracy of answers or decisions made. This record can be available to both the participant and the course leader, depending on the design of the courseware. This way, you can gauge the participant's progress and take whatever action progress or lack of progress may indicate.

There are two forms of interactive video: videotape and videodisk. Videotape is less expensive to produce but is slower to use due to its linear format; videodisk costs more to produce but is faster and more flexible due to its random-access nature. The trend seems to be toward videodisk. The main limitation to interactive video, other than cost, is availability of suitable courseware.

Special ingredients required include:

- Videodisk or Videotape Player, capable of being controlled by a personal computer
- Personal Computer
- Video Monitor
- An Interface, allowing the personal computer to control the monitor and the video equipment
- Suitable Courseware
- Personal Computer Software

INDIVIDUAL LEARNING EXPERIENCES (cont.)

III. **Personal Computer** — Another high-tech approach to individual learning. While it lacks the video impact of interactive video (the images seen are computer-generated), it is almost as versatile. It is an excellent vehicle for practice of a repetitive nature such a typing or reading skills course and is capable of providing simulations for operating a business, managing a project, doing financial analyses and "what-if" projections, and so forth. The limiting factor is availability of suitable software for the specific learning you want to take place, but this is improving rapidly.

Special ingredients required are:

- A Personal Computer, with sufficient memory and data storage for the application
- A Video Monitor
- Software, for the application
- Additional Instructions, related to the assignment, if any

INDIVIDUAL LEARNING EXPERIENCES (cont.)

IV. Personal Logbook/Journal — This is a personal learning tool which can help the individual get maximum benefit from assigned readings and in-class and out-of-class activities. It can be an important element of a life-long learning process because it encourages the habit of viewing every encounter with the written word, with a person or with an experience as an opportunity to learn something new. Through the log or journal, the individual can make connections between what he or she is learning and his or her own experiences and observations; think in terms of future applications, and use it as a basis for dialogue with others. Entries could include:

- A summary of the important points contained in a reading
- An argument, pro or con, about some particular point or points
- Notes to a colleague pointing out significant items of interest
- Thoughts about how to put the idea into practice
- Questions raised in the individual's mind

And a host of other things.

The ingredients for this are very simple:

- Learning Opportunities
- A Loose-Leaf Notebook with paper
- A Pencil or Pen
- The Desire to Learn from every experience

A Final Word of Encouragement

Well — a lot of ground has been covered — yet we've only scratched the surface. There are many techniques to help you be more effective in your role of course leader and much has been written on the topic. Use *The Course Leader's Cookbook* as a starting point. As you gain more experience, seek out additional information, study it, try it out in your classes, keep adding it to your tool kit. Soon you'll be creating your own "culinary masterpieces."

How Am I Doing?

(This questionnaire may be reproduced.)

My objective in conducting these classes is to provide you with a positive learning experience, one which provides you with useful information, concepts and techniques. It's important for me to know "how I'm doing." Your honest and candid answers to these questions will help me to help you. Please answer each question and return this form to me by _____ . This feedback covers the classes you attended on _____ .

(Course Leader)_____

For each question check one answer.

1. How effective was the Course Leader in presenting the material?
    - ☐ Very Effective
    - ☐ Somewhat Effective
    - ☐ Somewhat Ineffective
    - ☐ Not at all Effective

2. The Course Leader explained new ideas by relating them to familiar concepts.
    - ☐ Often
    - ☐ Most of the Time
    - ☐ Sometimes
    - ☐ Not Enough
    - ☐ Seldom

	Always	Quite Often	Sometimes	Seldom	Never

3. The Course Leader presented material at a level appropriate for me. ☐ ☐ ☐ ☐ ☐

4. The Course Leader explained the underlying rationale for particular techniques. ☐ ☐ ☐ ☐ ☐

5. How often did the Course Leader's personality interfere with learning? ☐ ☐ ☐ ☐ ☐

6. The Course Leader initiated fruitful and relevant discussions. ☐ ☐ ☐ ☐ ☐

7. The Course Leader encouraged me to express my opinion and experiences. ☐ ☐ ☐ ☐ ☐

8. The Course Leader pointed out what was important to learn in each class session. ☐ ☐ ☐ ☐ ☐

9. During the sessions, did the Course Leader check on participants' understanding? ☐ ☐ ☐ ☐ ☐

10. The Course Leader emphasized learning rather than tests or grades. ☐ ☐ ☐ ☐ ☐

11. The Course Leader varied the tempo of the class to suit content and participant needs. ☐ ☐ ☐ ☐ ☐

12. Was a good balance of student participation and Course Leader contribution achieved? ☐ ☐ ☐ ☐ ☐

Strongly Disagree
Disagree
Agree
Strongly Agree

13. The Course Leader talks too much about himself/herself. . ☐☐☐☐

14. The Course Leader seemed to sense when participants did not understand. .... ☐☐☐☐

15. The Course Leader promoted an atmosphere conducive to work and learning. .... ☐☐☐☐

16. The Course Leader attempted to involve all participants in classroom activities. .... ☐☐☐☐

17. The Course Leader was receptive to differing viewpoints and opinions.
    ☐ Yes, Quite Often
    ☐ Took Some Convincing
    ☐ Was Accepting
    ☐ Difficult to Convince
    ☐ No, Quite Closed Minded

18. Additional comments:

Name (optional)_____

About the authors ...

After 14 years at GE's Management Development Institute (Crotonville) in Croton-on-Hudson, New York, **Richard D. Colvin** formed The Learning Experience in 1984. While a Program Manager at Crotonville, Dick designed, developed, marketed and managed the Foreman/Supervisor Program which has been used by more than 7,000 foremen and first-line supervisors, worldwide, since 1970. He also designed the train-the-trainer course for the program, trained more than 500 operating managers to lead it at their plants, and conducted various GE management courses for more than 5,000 managers in the U.S. and nine other countries.

A graduate of Rutgers University who has also done graduate work at Fairleigh Dickinson University, Dick has had articles published in *Training Magazine* and the *Training and Development Journal*, is a member of the American Society for Training and Development (ASTD), American Consultants League (ACL) and is listed in *Who's Who in the East*.

Naomi C. Steinberg has been with General Electric since 1970. She joined GE's Technical Education Operation (TEO) as a training consultant in 1983 and has managed the Technical Management Course, the Manufacturing Concepts Course and the nine-course distributed Manufacturing Leadership Curriculum. The latter two programs were developed as part of GE's two-year, entry-level Manufacturing Management Program (MMP). Naomi currently manages TEO's Engineering and Manufacturing Operations Course (EMOC) and is heavily involved in designing and leading other TEO courses.

Previously, she was on the professional staff of GE's Management Development Institute (Crotonville). At Crotonville, she was responsible for a wide variety of activities ranging from program management to course leadership. She was also instrumental in the design and development of a generic Course Leadership Seminar and ran course leader training for many Crotonville programs, both in the U.S. and abroad.

Naomi, a graduate of Pace University in New York, is a member of the American Society for Training and Development (ASTD).